BECOMING a TEACHER

A Practical and Political School Survival Guide

Robin Gr Judy Kramer

D1362331

EDINFO
PRESS

ERIC® Clearinghouse on Reading, English, and Communication

Published 1993 by
ERIC Clearinghouse on Reading, English,
and Communication
Carl B. Smith, Director
2805 East 10th Street, Suite 150
Bloomington, Indiana 47408-2698
and
EDINFO Press
117 E. 6th Street
Bloomington, Indiana 47408

Editor: Warren Lewis
Design: Lauren Gottlieb
Cartoons: Dave Coverly
Production: Lauren Bongiani Gottlieb, Theresa Hardy
Cover: David J. Smith

ERIC (an acronym for Educational Resources Information Center) is a national network of 16 clearinghouses, each of which is responsible for building the ERIC database by identifying and abstracting various educational resources, including research reports, curriculum guides, conference paper, journal articles, and government reports. The clearinghouse on Reading, English, and Communication (ERIC/REC) collects educational information specifically related to reading, English, journalism, speech, and theater at all levels. ERIC/REC also covers interdisciplinary areas, such as media studies, reading and writing technology, mass communication, language arts, critical thinking, literature, and many aspects of literacy.

This publication was prepared with funding from the Office of Educational Research and Improvement, U.S. Department of Education, under contract no. RI88062001. Contractors undertaking such projects under government sponsorship are encouraged to express freely their judgment in professional and technical matters. Points of view or opinions, however, do not necessarily represent the official view or opinions of the Office of Educational Research and Improvement.

Library of Congress Cataloging-in-Publication Data

Grusko, Robin, 1947-
    Becoming a teacher : a practical and political school survival guide /
by Robin Grusko and Judy Kramer.
       p.   cm.
    ISBN 0-927516-37-3
    1. First year teachers—United States. 2. Teaching. 3. Classroom management—United States. I. Kramer, Judy, 1946-   . II. Title.
LB2844.1.N4G78   1993
371.1'02—dc20
                                 93-5409
                                   CIP

Table of Contents

Welcome!

Hello, new teacher! This book has a single purpose: to help you become the teacher you want to be.

New teachers are too often unable to negotiate the new environment of the school in which they find themselves for two reasons: They do not know the right questions to ask, and they do not know the right people of whom to ask them. This book supplies you—the new teacher—with the reassurance and encouragement, laughter and cautions that are the ingredients for success in teaching.

This is the book we wish we had read when we began our careers as new teachers.

Our book is not a hodge-podge compendium of instructional techniques—you got plenty of that in your Education courses. Neither do we propose a set of rules which, if followed, will automatically get you re-hired and tenured. Nor do we present a cut-and-dried formula for classroom success.

Rather, we tell the truth about what it's really like to become a teacher in a school. We advise you, we laugh and cry with you, we lay down caveats about some of the known mine fields, we talk realistically about the human relations of teaching, and we buoy up the idealism with which—we hope—you, as a new teacher, are filled. No matter whether you are teaching (or about to teach) in a public school or private school; a traditional school or an alternative school; an elementary, middle, or secondary school, the highly political culture inside the schoolhouse requires that you become savvy fast if you are to survive and succeed. We have survived, and we became successful; so have others; so can you.

If you are either a first-year or second-year teacher, or an Education major in your final year of teacher preparation, or a "second career" teacher or a teacher returning to school after a professional hiatus, then we are talking to you. Or, perhaps it's summertime and you are an untried new teacher awaiting that first day of school when you walk through those doors and down the hall to your very own classroom for the first time—this book is for you. With equally warm wishes, we write this book for you if you are a teacher with a few years of classroom experience who feels overburdened, overworked, and underloved.

We believe that you can successfully navigate the corridors of the school into which you have wandered—adjust to the school bureaucracy, overcome the undertow of your less-than-collegial colleagues, dodge the missiles of irate parents, and survive even a roomful of 35 kids—and find happiness at the same time. We believe this because we did it, and if we did it, so can you.

We are two teachers who have, between us, twenty-five years of experience teaching. Our schools are in a small urban district, thirty miles north of New York City. Judy teaches social studies; Robin teaches English. Moreover, we have had teaching jobs in many other situations—urban, rural, suburban; rich, poor; public, private; standard and traditional, alternative and innovative.

Our friendship and this book have evolved out of our desire to become excellent teachers. The old saw: "It takes five years to become a good teacher" seems to be true. What isn't true is that pain and anxiety must accompany those five years. We have accumulated many insights into the process of "becoming a teacher," and, along the way, we have discarded many of our old misconceptions, some of which we were taught in the Schools of Education. We wrote this book to help you become an accomplished teacher in less time than we took and with greater pleasure than we experienced.

We offer this book to you as a description of "school culture"—the physical, social, and psychological, human context in which you will be doing your teaching. These grand terms translate into such small concerns as: "Where do I hang my coat?" or "I don't have a file cabinet!" They imply the larger issues, as well: "Who has the real power in this school? How do I find out? What do I do with the knowledge once I have it?"

We have organized the book according to a framework that emerged naturally from our individual experiences, our dialogue with one another, and our conversations with other teachers. In six chapters—*Beginnings, Spaces, Rhythms, Systems, Kids,* and *Rewards*—we have discoursed with you as honestly as we could about our own and others' teaching successes and woes. We started writing this book during our joint study-hall assignment at our present school, and we developed it during joke-filled but intense discussions about how to get tenure.

In "Beginnings," we offer help to get a new teacher started with a new job in a new school.

In the "Spaces" chapter, we employ an anthropological model of the school culture in an attempt to help you get the lay of the land of your physical and social surroundings.

In "Rhythms," we show you how to adjust to the pace, the beat, the pulse of life in your school—the school day and year are highly rhythmic, you will find.

In chapter four, "Systems," we get honest about the bureaucracy—how it works and doesn't work, how it helps you and doesn't help you, and how you can learn to live with it and let it work for your own good and that of your students.

"Kids" is about your students—the reason why you're there.

The final section, "Rewards," comprises a lot of the best tips we have accumulated to keep the classroom alive, interesting, and fun for teachers and students alike, so that you can survive, will be soul-satisfied, and will enjoy success. There's more than one kind of reward in teaching.

We affirm that teaching is among the most valuable and honorable of professions. We thought so when we were new teachers, and we continue to think so. Since before the time of Socrates, great teachers have established the codes and methods of our profession. All human cultures accord special status and respect to their teachers. From the gurus who have been the spiritual teachers of India to the griots of Africa who recount the oral histories of their peoples, from the scholars of China to the law-givers and prophets of Israel and Jesus and his disciples, from e Scholastics of the Middle Ages to the *philosophes* of the European Enlightenment, from the scholars of the 19th century to you, the world's teachers are the foundation stones of every culture. As a teacher, you are following in that great, world-wide tradition.

You have probably been trained in only one approach to teaching, the one popular among your professors. Perhaps you have been fortunate enough to notice other styles of teaching available in our culture or teaching the way it is done in other cultures. Throughout the 20th century, high-minded philosophers, educational crusaders, faddists and highly paid consultants, and legislators and government bureaucrats have tried to reform schools. Each reform movement has swept through American education offering its patents as panacea for all of our educational ills. Each new wave of reform has left behind itself—in addition to major disappointments—a set of code words, jargon-ridden definitions of the problems in our schools and their solutions.

In the second half of the 20th century, we have been treated to more educational jargon and partial solutions than ever before, ostensibly to "empower" teachers—including, among others, individualized teaching, the teacher as facilitator, affective teaching, effective teaching, multi-media teaching, team-teaching, collaborative teaching, and teaching clusters. A veritable **alphabet** soup of more gobbledegook than there are letters in the alphabet describe the several approaches to instruction, each of which has been ballyhooed as *the* one that would best educate our students: **a**uthentic **a**ssessment, **b**ack-to-**b**asics, **c**ompensatory education, **d**eschooling, **e**lectronic classrooms, **f**lexible scheduling, **GED**, **h**umanistic education, **i**nterdisciplinary education, **j**ournal writing, **k**ey this and **k**ey that, **l**earning **l**aboratories, **m**ainstreaming, **n**on-graded programs, **o**pen education, **p**ortfolio assessment, **Q** methodology, **r**elevant curriculum (what a commentary on the rest of the curriculum!), **s**tructured environments, **t**racking, **u**nified studies, **v**oucher system, **w**hole language, and x, y, z.

Thanks to social scientists and psychologists, we now have expert jargon to describe the absolutely "best methods" of learning, including inquiry learning, hands-on learning, and cooperative learning. In these latter days, the business community has decided to treat schools as workplaces and students as workers, so now we hear that we are all "accountable," that "product" is what counts, that we must "take ownership" of our tasks, and that test scores are "the bottom line."

We do not take issue with the content or intent of any of these descriptive terms, though we can hardly resist observing that, ironically, the "transformation of the schools" of the 1970s preceded the "crisis of the schools" of the 1980s. We merely wish to point out that substitution of lingo for learning, and jargon for mastery, interferes with the development of a teacher's skills, and it detracts from a teacher's real reason for teaching: helping students learn.

Knowledge is what counts—and caring: your caring that your students come to know the subject that you teach, and that they know how to find out what they do not know. Knowledge and caring together produce the personal passion you need to keep teaching, and they generate a self-sustaining intellectual passion in both you and your students for life-long learning. By combining your mastery of the basics of your subject area with the "best" of all the instructional cure-alls, your passion for knowing and caring and teaching will continue to grow throughout your entire career. You may occasionally restructure the form of your lessons, and you may find yourself reorganizing into teams of teachers or advisors, but you will still be teaching the basics and the insights of your subject area.

Save thyself, new teacher, by avoiding the jargon, the clichés, and the lingo. Instead, use this little book to learn to place high value on your own skills, knowledge of your subject, and your individual ways of relating to your students. Maintain your energy and enthusiasm by keeping in mind Henry Adams's idea that "a teacher affects eternity; he can never tell where his influence stops."

J IS FOR JUDY   R IS FOR ROBIN

Beginnings

New beginnings prompt high expectations and great fears alike. As a new teacher, you will be entering a bureaucratic institution. You can control your place in it if you learn at the beginning how it operates. This bureaucracy can affect everything: whether your blackboards get cleaned, whether you have textbooks for your students, and whether you are rehired for the next year. As a novice, you will be unsure of the nuances and gradations of your job. You may not know whom to ask for information, and indeed, sometimes it is not wise to ask for that information.

Your new beginnings at school tie you to that bureaucracy—the administration, the faculty, and the curriculum. In order to become a fine teacher, you must learn to operate within the school institution. New teachers tend to fantasize fabulous lessons with fabulous students, but in isolation from the larger school community. Excellent teaching requires not only classroom skills but also political skills.

Most of us who become teachers do so out of idealistic good will and a desire to help young people learn and grow to be productive, thinking people. Some of us want a job that provides a sense of helping others. Others teach because teaching is a generally secure job with a perceived shorter working day. Still others have a love and zest for the subjects that they teach. Many of us carry mental models of our own "best" remembered teachers into the classrooms with us, and we try to emulate them. We look for students whom we see as being just as we were, or we look for "diamonds in the rough," or we try to educate those who have difficulty learning. We are all driven by combinations of images and needs, and we all probably bring more-or-less "all of the above" with us into our classrooms. But no matter what may have motivated you to become a teacher, if you don't develop skill—"wisdom in means"—at playing the bureaucratic game of school survival, you will be frustrated.

B IS FOR BEGINNINGS

This first chapter is about your getting started successfully. Read the next few pages, and you can open that wide heavy school door on the first day with greater ease, a firmer hand, and a lighter heart.

ENCOUNTERS OF THE FIRST KIND

Initially, you may assume that all materials—books, a desk, a file cabinet, and—if you're lucky—file cabinets, will come to them who wait. Not so! It's up to you to equip yourself.

The first questions that should be on your lips after you are told the magic words, "You're hired!" must be: "What books do I need?" and "Where can I get them?" If you were hired in June, take advantage of the summer months to gather and read all your resources. If, unluckily, you were hired in late August—an all-too-frequent last-moment act of bureaucratic desperation by those who hired you—you will need to put all your skills to use.

It is important to know whom to ask for the materials you need. The most logical person is often your immediate supervisor, such as the department chair or the principal or the assistant principal. These people will be those who evaluate your performance. Be cordial, be eager, put your best foot forward.

Books

In order for you to plan your courses efficiently, you must try to get all the materials you will need for at least the first months of school. Any book that the students need, you also need—preferably, two copies: one for school, one for your home office. You will need a large briefcase for all your papers; you certainly do not need to have a second briefcase for books. If your district will not provide you with two copies of each book, then smile and be accommodating! Thereafter, wait for the moment when you give the students their texts and unobtrusively help yourself to another copy for yourself. Do try to avoid lugging books back and forth from home to school.

Joe, a young student teacher, was assiduous and careful. He carried two large briefcases and walked at a running sprint through the halls. He thought he looked very professional and very "together." In fact, the opposite was true. Other teachers remarked that he looked frazzled and overburdened. Seasoned teachers know that pacing is critical to good teaching. Over-excitement leads to belly-flops.

You do not want to appear to work too hard; a goody-goody is never appreciated. You may, in fact, work hard. and we hope you do, but, as they say in Hollywood, "Never let them see you sweat!"

Desks, File Cabinets, and Rooms

What about all those other kinds of resources that you will need: a desk, a file cabinet, and how about a room? Do you even *have* a room? If you do, do you know where it is? Many new teachers start off in a school with five classes and five rooms, but not a file cabinet in sight. You will need a place to store each day's lessons, a place of easy access for old and future materials.

What do you do in a situation like that? Speak to your department chairperson or whoever is your immediate supervisor, remembering always to speak gently and with discretion. If you have developed a working relationship with an experienced teacher, quietly ask him or her how you can get some file space or whether teachers may change classrooms with each other.

If you find that a file cabinet is not available, or that your classroom situation cannot be changed, smile and wait. Again, do not let any distress cross your face in a public setting. As the new teacher, you are well advised to remember that you are being tested not only in terms of your classroom performance but also in other areas that may not be initially obvious. Discretion and initiative will get you through your first days—years—of teaching!

SCHOOL STAFF

On the day you go in to get your books, get to know all the "staff people" who really control the school mechanism.

Let's define our terms. Regardless of what you may have heard, there are no *unimportant* people in schools. A school is a finely tuned piece of machinery that needs oil on all its parts in equal amounts in order to run smoothly and efficiently. Sometimes the biggest machine can come to a grinding halt on account of the smallest cog. Do not spare the oil! All parts are equal when it comes to needing oil.

The Principal's Assistant

Introduce yourself immediately to the principal's secretary or administrative assistant. Take note of the title—if she is called "assistant," don't ever use the word "secretary." Titles are important to the people who wear them!

If you have not been given a tour of the school, you need one. Perhaps the principal's assistant can arrange one for you. Ask her; be tactful, however. Don't say: "Can you arrange a tour?" She may be busy; she may be thinking that it is not her job to act as your guide. Or, it may simply be a bad day for her. Say: "I haven't really seen the school yet. Is it all right if I walk around by myself? I would like to see where my room is, where the faculty lounge is," etc. etc. This will allow the Principal's Assistant a range of options for response. Be open and friendly; cash in on being a neophyte.

When Sarah began a job at one of her various high schools, she had no idea where the faculty room was. She had no idea where the English office was or even if there was one. She had been so enraptured with getting the job that she had forgotten to ask these important questions. The first day of school dawned, and as she entered the school, she realized that while she knew where her first class would be, she had no idea where to retreat, where to find her colleagues, or where to sit and work when she was on a prep period. These were questions that she should have asked earlier on reconnoitering missions.

The Copy Room and the Audio-Visual Personnel

Whom should you get to know? Eventually, everyone, but some people are essential to you from the very beginning.

You must get to know the people in charge of the audio-visual materials. You must get to know the people who take care of the reproduction equipment, materials, and services. These people can be critical elements in your success or failure at your new school. Find out who does the tasks at your school, and go see them, introduce yourself, and be pleasant! Your lessons are often at their mercy.

The audio-visual person, for example, is the technical genius who can save you from being observed by your supervisor while you fumble at the controls of a recalcitrant film projector. The person in charge of the copy machine, for another example, is the one who can get your materials copied in a last-minute rush on that morning after you have stayed up until one or two o'clock getting ready for your big evaluation. If you have already made friends with these people, they'll be a friend when you need one.

The Custodian

Another person critical to your survival is the custodian of your building. He may be the only person who knows what is going on everywhere and all the time. Get to know his name. Make sure you wave the flag of cordiality in front of him. You do not want him to go spewing forth about your lack of control with your fourth-period writing group. How does he know that they nearly had you in tears last Tuesday? Unbeknownst to you, he was repairing a leaky faucet outside the windows of your room.

Never underestimate the power of the support people whose quiet work often goes unacknowledged, but whose efforts are essential to a smoothly functioning school. A kind word, a bright smile, a generous and genuine interest in their lives may save your own life one day.

The Administration and Its Many Arms

In any feudal institution, such as schools, there are fiefdoms with guarded entrances and exits that are carefully controlled. Be aware of their existence; learn who has the keys! School teaching is a real-life game of "Dungeons and Dragons," but without preternatural powers.

During those first few days of school, you must build bridges to the Administration. First of all, get to know the organizational flow, and understand the breakdown of the several administrators' particular duties in your school.

David was working in a school with rigid boundaries between the duties of the department chairs and the principals. Before school started that first year, he went into school on a reconnoitering expedition, and he met the principal, whom he had not seen since his hiring interview two months before. She cordially showed David about the school, and she invited him to come to see her whenever he had a question.

A IS FOR ADMINISTRATION

A few days later, he was speaking to his chairperson, happily relating this encounter to him. The chairperson gently informed David that any questions he might have were to be directed to himself, and that the principal, for the most part, stayed behind closed doors. The department chair—as he made perfectly clear to David—was his immediate superior, not the principal.

We advise: Find out before school begins who your direct supervisor is. This person will write your evaluation.

Other administrators whom you need to know are the assistant principals. They are often the ones in charge of discipline. Learn the discipline system in your school and the guidelines for disciplinary referrals. You may have learned about these in an orientation session, if you're lucky enough to be in a progressive school district that has anything as radically useful as an orientation session. If you're on your own, then go to the trouble to greet and meet this person, or these persons, during your reconnoitering mission before the advent of the first day of school. Learn their names, and let them know who you are.

Knowing procedures before you need them is healthy and wise; new teachers are often judged at a snap by the control they maintain over their classes. Therefore, always try to handle a problem on your own before asking for help from an administrator. The walls of a school have eyes and ears which often are invisible to the novice. You want them to like what they are hearing and seeing.

Guidance Counselors, Social Workers, School Psychologists

Though you may not need them on Day One, the guidance counselors, the social workers, and the school psychologists are not to be forgotten on your early travels though the school. These people often know your rep before you even become aware that there is "a morning line" on you. Honor them with an introduction, and cause them to know that you understand why they are important. These folks often feel that they are the most hardworking, and the most misunderstood, staffers in the school. Understand, if you want to be understood.

We advise: Stand back, observe quietly, come to know which counselors can help both you and your students. Always be cooperative and on time in meeting their requests.

The Aides: Hall, Teacher, Attendance

Other important school personnel whom you must not forget to meet are the aides—hall, teacher, and attendance. These people have an ubiquitous presence in a school. Hall aides hear the gossip in the halls from the students; they know which teacher is a pushover, which teacher is tough, and which teacher is liked or disliked. We do not say that the information they hear or transfer to others is accurate. Their slant may be totally distorted, but it must not be discounted. Make your alliances with the aides early on. Be cordial and be pleasant. Your effectiveness as a teacher rests to a great extent on the support and cooperation of everyone in the school, including the lowest aide on the totem pole.

PROCEDURES ARE IMPORTANT

Find out the procedures in all the teacher-support areas; learn them and follow them. Do not, in your first year, initiate any ideas about new ways to do the job. Very likely, the people who run these areas have been there for a long while; they understand the ins and outs better than you do.

Initially, make sure that you get your requests in on time. Give the people fulfilling them a few days; try not to have any rush jobs until you have an established working relationship.

Never complain about any school personnel either in their presence or to a third party at school. Keep your complaints to yourself about any school staffer, until you understand the lay of the land, which may take a year or more. Either swallow your complaints or take them home: Tell your mother, your father, your sister, your brother, your spouse, or your cat or goldfish, but no one else. Teaching is living in a small world in which everything that goes around, comes around.

If it happens that you are teaching in a small, suburban or rural district, be aware that your teaching world is even tinier than that of a large urban school district. Your next-door neighbor may be the school-board president's sister! You are a new member of a long-standing society. Establishing your own proper, comfortable position in this community will take time.

PLANNING LESSONS BEFORE THE START OF SCHOOL

You're OK! You have your books; you know where your room is or rooms are; you scored a file cabinet; and you have met some of the important people on your minor planet. What next?

Don't just stand there; it's time to hit those books! You have to prepare some lessons, organize your teaching week into manageable units, and take a few deep breaths. Guideline sheets for the students about your expectations regarding their work, their books, their behavior in your class—all of this is as important for you as it is for them. Now is the time—before school starts—for you to sit down to write these sheets out. Remember: You want to get them to the copy machine long before the first day of school.

What will you say to your students that first day?

Plan exactly what you will do on the first day and on the second and third days of that first week, too. Even if you don't do in detail as you had planned, you need to be well-armed.

Now, in plenty of time before it all starts up, is the right time for you to sit down and plot out your strategies thoughtfully. You may be asked to show lesson plans to your supervisor at some point, too. If so, don't panic. It is standard school procedure for a chairperson to become a mentor to the new teachers. The chair who hired you will certainly have an interest in your success. Your success is your chairperson's success. As a new teacher, remember that you do not have all the answers. The wise new teacher is one who is able to take criticism, both positive and negative, with alacrity; the wise new teacher is also one who is able to take that criticism and use it.

You are going to have a lot to think about during your first few months of teaching: the kids, the courses, the planning, the grading, your evaluations, and (remember?) your personal life (if you still have one, by then). Even though you have now become a teacher, you remain a human being. Make your life easier in all respects: a few seconds or minutes of planning will save you hours of running!

OTHER NEWCOMERS

You probably will have been hired with other newcomers. Even though your tendency will be to form friendships among the newcomers, you may find that you are in an adversarial position with them. Do not naively assume that all new teachers who do a good job will be rehired. Enrollments decline, and old teachers return unexpectedly from leaves. You may find yourself pitted against other non-tenured newcomers for the few remaining positions.

Chris discovered upon entering his classroom that another new teacher, whom he had met in an orientation session and with whom he had developed a quick friendship, was being observed by an administrator. Anticipating that he would be next, Chris absentmindedly laid his notebook down on the desk, and took some deep breaths to relieve his stage fright. Chris had prepared an excellent lesson—a role-playing game with parts for each student. When the class began, he discovered, however, that his notebook was no longer on the desk. In desperation, Chris struggled to teach a lesson by using the bits and pieces of the game that he had saved in another notebook, but alas, the lesson was a fiasco. Afterwards, his colleague and "friend" said, "Oh, by the way, I must have taken your notebook by mistake." New teachers are often forced to compete with one another. Take care to protect yourself.

THE FACULTY

It is the first day of school. You have said your hellos to the secretary and to the custodian. You have given next week's handouts to the copy-room person. You have gotten your materials for the upcoming periods of the day, and you have even found your way to the faculty room for your first prep period. You want to do some last-minute preparation for your next class, but you do not want to seem rude to the friendly, inquiring stares of your new associates. What do you do?

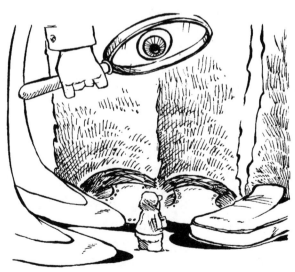

F IS FOR **FACULTY**

If you really wanted to do some serious work, you should not have gone into the faculty room in the first place. Some schools have designated specific rooms for work, and other rooms for conversation. Some schools have departmental offices, and in the best of all worlds, schools also have rooms for socialization, too.

Knowing where to go is is no less important than knowing what to do once you get there. If you have important work to do, and your school has but a single all-purpose room, what should you do? You can always go to the library; that seems to be the one spot in a school where you can usually find peace. You can also search the halls for an empty classroom—ask the school scheduling person, or the custodian, for this information.

Uh oh! You've wandered into the teachers' lounge by mistake. You want to do some work, but it seems that no one else is working. What do you do? Find a quiet corner of the room? Open up your books? Say hello to all? Don't wait for someone to ask you who you are. Introduce yourself—you probably were one of hundreds vying for the job. You're important, even if you are the youngest or the newest faculty member on staff.

Expect people to be curious about you, but do not give away any part of yourself in the initial encounters. The teachers you meet may very well become your friends over the next few months, but at present, they are merely strangers. On the whole, school teachers tend to be a cliquish breed. You will need some time to assess the people around you before jumping headlong into anything approaching a personal relationship.

Let's get back to the quiet corner in which you have ensconced yourself. The introductions are over, the clock hand is sweeping quietly around, moving you towards your next class; you need to get some work done. Simply say so to the others. They will understand—they remember what it was like to be a new teacher, a story with which they will try to regale you many times before the year is out. They may laugh and smile condescendingly, but by and large, they will respect your need to have some quiet time. If they persist in talking to you, go with the flow—but keep your papers open. Try to work as you reply to their questions, but don't return there the next day!

FRIENDSHIPS

An important survival issue in your school is knowing to whom to speak, when to speak, and—most important perhaps—when to be silent.

The new teacher is often too eager to make new friendships. You will find friends, but you must find them slowly. Forge alliances carefully and knowingly.

Two teachers hired at the same time for the same subject became close friends as the year progressed. Each was free at the same times, and they each had the identical course load. They found out that they shared many commonalities in their private lives as well—each had two children of the same ages, each had an ex-husband, each was pondering an approaching second marriage. They both had been hired for tenure-track positions; both felt equally secure in their performance in the classroom. They shared ideas, lesson plans, despairs, and successes. April came—"the cruelest month of all"—and with it, they each hoped, a renewal of their contracts. The chairperson of their department called them in and spoke to them together: "I have one job for next year, but there are two of you. You both have done a fine job this year, but like Solomon, I must choose only one. In consultation with the school board's legal counsel, the principal and I have determined that the person who was hired first will get the job. The only way to determine this is to ascertain whose name was spoken first at the Board of Ed. meeting when you two were hired."

The teacher whose name began with the letter higher in the alphabet retained her job—an ironic twist of fate without regard to intelligence, performance, or aptitude. The friendship of these two teachers, moreover, did not endure the resulting bitterness and resentment incurred by these whimsies of the educational bureaucracy.

Orientation sessions for new staff members are excellent places to meet other new staff members. Another new teacher, one who is not in your department, can be a good friend and associate. Sometimes, teachers in the same departments or at the same grade level compete for praise, popularity, honors, and preferments. Seek out friends in another department or grade—someone who can help you evaluate your own work objectively, and will point out the pitfalls of teaching in your school, and not be your competitor.

Often, orientation sessions are ongoing throughout the year; they can offer many opportunities to share common interests and concerns. In-service courses run by your own district or neighboring ones are also excellent places to meet others. Because new teachers are often finishing courses for their state certification, you can network while you are completing the coursework.

Meeting others is relatively easy; knowing what to say once you meet them is sometimes more problematic. Jim was quickly befriended by another teacher in his department. September eased into October, and a real sense of simpatico developed between the two. Jim confided in his new friend that he was having some serious problems with one of his classes; he confessed that he was quite unsure about his effectiveness in getting the material across to the students, and one student in particular, Erica, was giving him a lot of flak.

Soon thereafter, Jim's supervisor asked for a conference to discuss the problems that Jim was having with his fourth-period class. During the conference, the chair asked Jim: "What are you doing about Erica's behavior?"

Jim's new-found "friend" had ratted. The chair could not have known about Erica any other way. Jim's trust had been misplaced.

As a new faculty member, you will be a subject of discussion and school-wide interest. Expect people to come up and offer you advice and support, but be wary! Measure the offers. Judge the depth of the water carefully, and do not plunge in capriciously.

T is for TEACHER

THE SCHOOL BOARD, PTA MEMBERS, PARENTS, AND YOU

In both large and small school districts, the new teacher's classroom door is never really closed. As a new teacher, you will be teaching to more eyes and ears than those attached to your students' heads. You need to learn to whom those unseen eyes and ears belong.

Every district publishes and distributes a calendar of the school year. The calendar usually contains the names of the members of the Administration, the School Board, and the Parent-Teacher Association. There may also be a telephone directory. Leaf through the calendar and other district publications, watching for family names that appear on your class rolls. Familiarize yourself with the faculty list, too. You may be teaching the children of politically powerful parents. Knowing your subject matter well is only part of keeping your job.

What do you do if the principal's daughter or the school-board president's son is in your class, and he or she refuses to do the homework you have assigned?

Do what you would do with any other person's daughter or son; do not change your modus operandi at all. Speak to the student. If that doesn't work, follow the procedures outlined in your particular district. If you are fair and unbiased in your evaluation, and if you have carefully documented the problem, then a parent will usually understand your position. No student should be given preferential treatment because his or her parent is "somebody." Meanwhile, document all conversations, notes sent home, and phone calls with parents.

MaryAnn was in her second year of teaching science in a small rural district. When she received her class lists in September, she realized, with dismay, that Delphine, a daughter of one of the most influential board members, was in her third-period class. MaryAnn had heard from other faculty members about Delphine: Delphine had posed both disciplinary and instructional problems to them all. To MaryAnn's relief, however, she and Delphine got along fine, although Delphine's writing ability was well under the standard for her level, and this information needed to be conveyed to her parents.

During the conference that MaryAnn arranged with Delphine's parents, MaryAnn showed them copies of their daughter's essays, explaining in a forthright manner what Delphine's problems were, and how she could be helped. MaryAnn followed Polonius' advice to Laertes in *Hamlet:* "This above all, to thine own self be true." MaryAnn knew that she could not live with herself were she to accept Delphine's mediocrity and give her grades that she did not deserve. The result was that Delphine's parents were charmed by MaryAnn's direct and honest approach; they believed that Dephine was really going to get the help in this English class that she had been needing for so long. From that point on, they became MaryAnn's staunchest supporters.

Give no student preferential treatment. The new teacher must not play favorites either by showering approval or by withholding disapproval. Knowledge of your subject field, and a clear perception of your students' problems, will abundantly and honorably prove your desire for helpful communication among yourself, your students, and their parents. Very often, the inexperienced teacher flounders in a parent conference because of lack of confidence.

P IS FOR **PARENTS**

We advise: Do what Mrs. Anna does in *The King and I:*

Whenever I feel afraid,
I hold my head erect
And whistle a happy tune,
So no one will suspect,
I'm afraid.

Feign the confidence that you may not feel, and often you can transfuse that confidence into your own veins.

THE CURRICULUM

What do you teach?

This may seem to be a really foolish question, but it often is one of the first questions that the new teacher has to answer.

Barry was hired in October to fill in for an English teacher who had become ill. "I was hired on Thursday and scheduled to begin on Monday. The department chair gave me the anthology that the class was using. There was neither a grammar book nor a vocabulary book. I was told that it was a ninth-grade general class. I was not given any guidelines other than to be told that the ninth-grade English course was a genre approach. Any decisions about the actual lessons were to be mine. This was really too much for me to handle. I wanted more guidance, but I received none. So I went home and, looking through the anthology, I came to a story that I had found exciting when I was in high school. Now, as the teacher, I told the kids why the story had been meaningful to me, and it made a hit in my classroom."

Situations like this one are quite often the rule rather than the rarity. What do you do when you are asked to perform outside your area of expertise? Do as Barry did. Teach your passion; find something that you enjoy. If you are enthralled by your material, then your students will catch their enthusiasm from you.

Your department chairperson is the one who will be overseeing your activities regarding curriculum. If there is no department chair, then there is usually an assistant superintendent or an assistant principal who is charged with this duty.

Try to understand exactly what the curriculum is, what must be taught, what is expected to be taught, and what is expected not to be taught. Sometimes, these pieces of information become clear only as the year progresses. Don't expect instant answers. Go slowly. Look to the others in your department as models.

Models: What about all those other teachers in your department who are teaching courses like yours, and have been teaching them for years? The new teacher often assumes that the old dogs will be happy to teach the young pups their tricks.

Don't count on it! Unfortunately for you, teachers can be altogether possessive about their ideas and their materials. If they have been working many years to develop their files on this unit or that novel or some other subject, you must undertand that they may be reluctant to deliver unto you the fruits of their labor.

If you think that some older teacher is likely to help, better to ask for a specific facet of a lesson plan, rather than the whole thing: e.g., a finely tuned composition assignment, a crossword puzzle that has all the words associated with your new unit, or a pithy magazine article that punctuates your point well.

Teachers are proud of their hard work and good lessons, and they often very willingly share bits and pieces of these with newcomers, but preferably on their own terms. Trading ideas is like trading baseball cards: It's give and take. Mention a good idea or a reference to someone in your department; more than likely, he or she will reciprocate with an idea or two for you. As always and on other matters, don't go overboard here, either.

One fine source for curriculum ideas and innovations is the professional organization for your discipline, e.g., the National Council of Teachers of English or the National Council for History Education. These organizations are there for you: join up; use their resources; subscribe to the professional journal for your subject, and read it diligently every month.

YOU HAVE ONLY JUST BEGUN

Teaching is not only a matter of managing your time. It is not only a matter of knowing and loving your subject matter. It is not only a matter of controlling your classes. All these are important, and you cannot be a satisfied or successful teacher without them, and this is what they taught you in your Education classes. What they don't teach you is how to understand the the Byzantine labyrinth of a school bureaucracy like the one that you are entering. When you step across the threshold of that school on your very first day, you have begun the journey of learning to become an excellent teacher, but you have only just begun.

SPACES

You got the job. Congratulations!

You have learned to whom to speak, and when. You have your books and your plans—no mean accomplishments! What next? Do you have a space of your own? Do you know how to deal with that space now that you have secured it?

The new teacher who has just gotten a new job is often so enamored of this accomplishment alone—and understandably, for it is a major accomplishment to get a job in this ever-competitive world of teaching—that he or she is often dreamily unaware of how the physical space of the new environment can alter one's personal space.

The successful beginner will learn that even though spaces shape who and what we are, it is also true that we shape our spaces. The culture of an institution such as a school can be significantly altered by its features, both architectural and human. This chapter is about learning to understand the new space you have found yourself in, and the new space that you are about to make for yourself.

A school is a bureaucratic institution whose vagaries can be controlled, and manipulated, if you understand them. Your space, in both the physical and the personal senses, in this bureaucracy can also be controlled by your taking a clever hand in fitting yourself in. The extent to which you can adjust and modify the social realities of your own space we term your "CQ"—your comfortability quotient. The higher your CQ in the new position, the higher will be your chances for success and happiness in your new career.

S IS FOR SPACES

THE PHYSICAL SPACE, or "All I Want Is a Room Somewhere"

The Classroom

Have you ever heard of an office where the new worker is told that he has a job, but he might not have a room or a desk or even a place to hang his coat? Have you ever heard of a situation where the new worker is told that, yes, he has an office, but that right now it is occupied by another person who might or might not be willing to share drawer space with him? This is often the scenario in the school setting.

How does the wary novice with a low CQ negotiate a way into a space of one's own?

The ideal, of course, is a whole room all your own. If you are given this, count your blessings, decorate it to the hilt, and enjoy! If you do not have a room of your own, ask to be introduced to the person with whom you will be sharing. This person will, no doubt, have all sorts of rules for you to follow: which drawer to use, the position of the window blinds, the desk set-up, who can hang what where.

What do you do if you are unhappy with all this?

The wise and successful teacher is often the person who can maneuver the waters at the trickiest of narrows. Once you are introduced to the "proud owner of the room," be sure to let your new roomie know that you do not want to upset the status quo (at least not initially). Those 25 posters that you purchased with your own money last summer and prepared with care and love? Leave them at home, for the time being. All those tattered, out-of-date posters hanging on the walls of this room to which you have been (grudgingly) admitted? Leave them there, even if they do not fit in with your courses. They may be that teacher's proudest possessions.

Ask first, regret not later. Tamper with somebody else's habitual sense of their own space at your own risk! Very often, the person who is to be your roommate will be pleasant and willing to share ideas, notes, personal exchanges, even wall space. Very often, however, the reverse is true. As the new teacher, you must be ready with the first gesture of accommodation and friendship. And don't be dismayed if your offers are refused; look elsewhere for collegial sharing. If your roommate turns out not to be the soulmate you dreamed of, do not despair; you may be assigned a mentor, or you may be involved in team-teaching. Meanwhile, follow your roomie's rules to the best of your ability.

Scenario: You have tried to follow the rules of the classroom; you have one class, however, that is a problem. The person with whom you share the room is a stickler for a clean desk; in fact, she has insisted from Day One that you do not leave any papers on her desk (never mind that it's your desk, too), and that all handouts and books be put away before you leave the room.

At the end of each class period, however, kids are always coming up to you with an assortment of complaints and requests. You have another class in another room immediately after this one; you are so busy with your students that you have no time to clean up the desk, talk to the students, and move to the next class where you will be teaching another subject. You leave the desk in a state of disarray that is the visible and outward expression of the disarray in your psyche. You get to the next class frazzled, you have not been able to negotiate your way successfully on any of the fronts you are dealing with: the student, the classroom teacher, your next class, and, of course, your own anxiety.

This is a common situation for the new teacher without a space of her own. What can you do?

We advise: Examine the situation to see where the problem began: Always look to the source. The source in this instance was the students who crowded your desk and your time after the class. Explain to the whole class—at a time when you are calm and well-ordered in soul—that you can no longer entertain their questions and concerns at the end of the period. Explain that you have a problem. (Students love it when their teachers have problems!) Explain that you need their help. (Students love it when you place yourself at their mercy!) Ask them to help you find a solution to your problem, remembering that there is hardly anyone quite so intelligent as a teenager. The odds are that they themselves will propose that you set up appointments to meet with them at other hours. Your students can become your greatest allies in your new space.

Office Space

The space of the secondary teacher is very different from the space of a teacher in an elementary school. In the lower grades, office space and classroom space are synonymous, but in most cases, most elementary teachers have a classroom. In a secondary school, however, the classroom is often not the teacher's office, and, in fact, the secondary teacher may not have a space that could be called an office. In this case, then, if the secondary teacher moves from room to room, sharing space with others, she may not have either a classroom or an office. Elementary teachers are luckier this way.

Question: What do we mean by "an office?"

Answer: An office is any space where individual, private work is done.

With this "working" definition (pun intended), we can generously suggest that EVERY secondary school teacher will have an office, since by the nature of the definition, the savvy teacher will find some space somewhere in the larger spaces of the bureaucracy to get the work done. Offices are where you find them.

O IS FOR OFFICE

The nature of your day as a school teacher will require that you have a number of preparation periods—they vary from school to school—in which to work, probably from space to space. This is not the ideal, of course; but, then, we do not concern ourselves with the ideal. Besides, you would not have needed us as your guides for the ideal. If you were given an office space with a phone, a desk, a file cabinet that locks, a chair (even two) and—unthinkable!—a secretary to type up your tests and quizzes, you'd know exactly what to do. It is the absence of these fine accoutrements to the good life with which the novice teacher needs help coping.

You need to know that you *can* be happy even without material possessions—a room of your own, a wall of your own, a desk of your own, a desk drawer of your own. Indeed, as a teacher, you have already embraced the promise of intangible rewards with which society rewards teachers. How, now, to live within the limits of your choices? Very often, schools have designated office spaces for each of their departments. If this is the case, then you will be given some amount of space in that office. You may have to share a desk or a file cabinet. There will likely be one phone for all.

We advise: Be wise, be savvy, don't whine. As the new kid on the block, you have to be less demanding and more flexible than the others. The new teacher who wants to keep school materials private will not keep any important tests or papers in a file cabinet or a desk that must be shared. Keep whatever space you are allotted clean and tidy, and don't leave papers lying about.

What about the new teacher who does not have even a shared desk? What about the new teacher who only has a locker in the same hall as the students—and who doesn't even know how to unlock that locker?

We advise: Find the biggest briefcase you can, appoint it with all the niceties of a fine office—stapler, clips, scissors, pens, pencils, rulers, tape, a pocket calculator—and carry it with you. You will soon earn the reputation of being an earnest and persevering person. Like the neighbor always willing to borrow a cup of sugar or one of your tools from the garage, fellow teachers will flock about in pursuit of your stapler, clips, scissors, pens, pencils, rulers, tape, and that calculator. Whatever you do, do not brag about your wonderful ability to conquer the odds. Win demurely, speak softly, and carry a big briefcase.

HOME SPACE

The best solution for all of your office space needs is to set up an office in your home.

A wise investment for the new teacher is the purchase of a filing cabinet and a desk. Hint: Keep only one hard copy of all your handouts in a file folder; class sets can be cumbersome, especially if you do not have a school office. In your home office, you can also keep the second set of textbooks that we recommended earlier; this obviates the need to carry books back and forth with you. The other advantage of a home office is that you do not have to worry about the security of your files and books. The only eyes and hands that will touch your things are your own. Very often, in the school work space, handouts and books have a way of walking away.

Dennis and Melissa shared a room in a high school without office space for either of them. Dennis was always prepared; Melissa lived "on the edge." Dennis said to Melissa, "I'll be glad to share my handouts with you any time; just let me know in advance." One day, Dennis, the organized teacher, had a set of class papers that had been stacked on his desk for later in the week. Why were the papers lying on the desk? He had no file cabinet at school and had no place to store them at home.

Melissa had a schedule similar to Dennis's, and when she saw the material, and she didn't have a lesson prepared, as was her wont, she helped herself to the class set that was waiting for David's upcoming lesson. When David arrived, he looked frantically for his handouts, but lo and behold, they were gone. He confronted Melissa. With alacrity, she said that, yes, she had used them for her class, but why was David so upset since, after all, he had extended to her an invitation to use his materials any time! The moral of this story is that you must set up your own space, both at school and at home, so that it serves you best; and, be careful what you offer.

STORAGE SPACE

The migratory school teacher, who moves about from room to room, needs to become a strange animal: a cross between a camel and an octopus. You will need strong legs to carry you through your day; sitting will become an extinct social custom. Your eight arms will help you to produce and carry all your stuff.

We have already mentioned drawer space and desk space; the locked file cabinet is a wonderful accessory to add to your teaching wardrobe.

Warning: Lose the key, and you may never find another! Schools are notorious for their inability to have more than one key per item.

One teacher we know lost the key to her file cabinet; the janitor came to her aid by ripping open the cabinet with a large metal implement, thereby rendering the cabinet useless for its intended purpose and considerably shortening its natural life. The drawers were still able to open and even to close, but locking them was impossible.

When you are given keys, always try to make duplicates. If they are the kind of keys that cannot be duplicated, be very careful. The teacher who is successful is often the one who knows where the keys are.

If you are given a file cabinet, and you suspect that another teacher has keys to it, do not put anything in it that you are afraid of losing. Sharing is a wonderful thing, and we have all been taught to share since we were kindergartners; nevertheless, sharing is sharing when we freely give. Sharing is not sharing when something is taken from you.

Beyond books, handouts, and files of lessons, what do you do with personal items: coat, boots, umbrellas? If you begin your job in September—and you teach in a climate where most days are warm—questions about these items do not come up for a while. If winter makes the isssue important, you may be embarrassed to have to ask: "Where do I put my coat?" Find out the answer to this question of storing personal items at the beginning. Carrying your coat around with you helps to promote the wrong image—that of someone who is out of control.

Besides, jackets and coats and especially umbrellas have a way of disappearing if they are not locked up safely.

WORK SPACE

The ideal is often not the real, and that goes double for school teachers. Especially for high-school teachers, work space is limited, and privacy is at a minimum. Prep time is short, and the paperwork engendered by the school bureaucracy may well eat up any work time that you find you do have. Even if you were to find a bit of time for work, you probably have no cozy spot in which to do it, so everything evens out.

Do not expect to do any really serious preparations for your courses during the day at school. A realistic expectation is that you will be able only to correct papers and REVIEW the notes and plans that you have ALREADY prepared. As it has already been established that you are the average school teacher in the average school in an average town, get used to the idea that you will probably have neither office nor desk nor time; you must prepare your lessons elsewhere and elsewhen.

As a beginning teacher, you are going to have a lot to do: planning lessons; grading papers; reviewing the course work; filling out forms for the guidance office, the principal, the school secretary, to name a few of the personnel who will make claims upon your time. And we have not even mentioned the students, yet! Do find some time for them during the day, if you can; students have a funny way of intruding into your time as teacher.

True story: Anna became so involved in planning a lesson during her prep period one day that she didn't hear the bell ring for the class. The next thing she did hear was the bell tolling the end of class. Where had Anna been? Not in her classroom! What had Anna's students been doing during the time when she was absent preparing her perfect lesson for them? Not being perfect! What did the administration say upon hearing of Anna's earnest, but preoccupied, desire for the perfect lesson? The principal made the obvious comment that a perfect lesson becomes perfect only when it has been used by both the teacher *and* the students, not when it remains in the teacher's notebook.

Keep your priorities straight: Your students come first. When do you find time to plan and grade and review and do other work? When do you find time to do all the necessary tasks of the beginning teacher? Never—or almost never—at school.

Sundays are excellent days on which to do school work. (And students think that they are the only ones with heavy homework assignments!) Teaching is not a nine-to-five job; you may have to work on the weekends and on school nights. And yes, your family—itchy spouse, begging children, waiting dogs, and resentful cats—may sometimes complain, and they do sometimes get angry and sometimes fail to understand.

Nevertheless, teaching is, and shall remain, a vital part of the fabric of your life. Even though work space and work time at school may be at a minimum, as a beginning teacher, your work itself will not be minimal. You will have to find working time and working space that work for you, and that means at home, not at school, and on your own time, not school time.

CLOSED/OPEN SPACE

Beginning teachers tend to think that they can go into their classrooms, close the doors, and teach. However, there are no "closed doors" in a school. Students are not inanimate creatures who do not speak (although you may sometimes think that they are animate non-thinking creatures who never stop talking). Students have mouths, classroom doors lead to hallways, walls adjoin other rooms. Whatever happens in your room that is the least bit noteworthy—other than the coursework—will be grist for the gossip mills.

Moreover, just as everything that happens inside your room flows out, so also anything outside can come in. You will be subject to continual evaluations; your supervisors will think that they can walk into your room at any time, and that is their right.

During Walter's first days at his school, he was amazed to see one teacher, who had about five years of experience, teaching with her door open. Walter would look into her room and be quite amazed that she could teach so openly; after all, wasn't teaching a clandestine, intimate affair between master and disciples? During his trips to and from the faculty room, Walter glanced in through his colleague's door, saw it all, and learned a lot: On some days, the students worked quietly in small groups, while the teacher walked around easily among the desks; on other days, the students seemed to be screaming all at once, and the teacher seemed to be allowing it, quite openly. She never closed her door, even during the most raucous moments.

One day, one of Walter's most difficult classes got out of hand during a review session—they were all talking at once, and some were screaming; they were getting up from their seats and milling about the room; they were doing all the things that "good teachers" never allow their students to do. Walter looked at the closed door, said a silent prayer of thanks for his sagacity in having closed it before class started, and then he went back to trying to quiet his students down.

An increasingly competent teacher, Walter managed, somehow, to restore order before the bell rang. Thinking the incident was as closed as his door had been, Walter forgot all about that afternoon. Some days later, however, Walter was on the carpet for lacking the skills of a disciplinarian. His department chairperson had been walking through the halls that day, and because Walter's door had been closed, the chair had not been able to see Walter at his desk regaining control. The chair had heard only the noise, but he had not been able to see Walter doing what needed to be done. Had Walter's door been open, the chairperson could have seen him. The irony is that the closed door did not keep the noise inside or the appropriately nosey chairperson outside. The closed door was a detriment, not an advantage.

D IS FOR DOOR

We advise: Get comfortable with an open-door policy. Be relaxed about being observed at your work without warning. Go ahead and stage an extravaganza for the occasions when you know ahead of time that **THEY** are coming to observe, and you are going to be evaluated. But also know that if you are always working at the top of your abilities, if you are always doing your best, an earnestness will shine through. Super-duper lessons that we concoct may very well look and sound phony, anyway. Be natural, do your best, and you will succeed in the open environment of your open-door classroom.

You will not be able to plan for every contingency in life. What you can do is prepare to be unprepared; in that case, you will be ready for anything.

SPACES TO GO, PLACES TO SEE

The Lunch Space

When is lunch time? Where do we eat?

Lunch space in schools is usually at a premium, so there are usually multiple lunch periods during the day. In some large high schools, the cafeteria(s) may be open throughout the day. This will have an impact upon your teaching because students walking through the halls outside YOUR ROOM have food on the brain, not studies. You will need to know how to deal with these loud noises that distract both you and your students.

Where and when do the teachers eat? Is there a teacher's cafeteria, or do the teachers eat in the faculty room? Is there a refrigerator for the teachers? What about the working lunch? Will one of your classrooms be free during your lunch period? These are all important questions to which you need to seek answers.

During the first, lonely year of teaching, eat well. Teachers do not live by lesson plans alone.

Personal Space

Although the several spaces of the physical plant of your school may have more control over you than you have over them, your personal space and your demeanor are variables that you can control. Your students and colleagues will often evaluate you by your appearance. Take time to look smart; it will contribute to your sense of self-control and control of the space around you. You can unilaterally bring about the atmosphere you wish to project. Find your place by making it!

Hiding Space

Into each teacher's day some rain may fall. What do you do if you have no room, no desk, no place to call your own, no umbrella from school rain? What do you do if the only place to go during your preparation periods is the faculty lounge, that big brawling place filled with curious eyes? What do you do on the day that your Significant Other leaves you? On the day that your children are sick (not sick enough to stay home, only sick enough to engender the possibility that their school nurse might call you)? On the day that you feel the migraine of your life coming on because you lost a set of graded essays? What do you do when you need to find a quiet space of your own in the complex world of the jungle where you teach?

H IS FOR HIDING PLACE

Simple answer to complex questions: You go to the Hiding Place that you searched for on an earlier reconnoitering mission throughout your building, discovered, and have been holding in readiness.

Do not use the rest rooms for this purpose; they are useful only for brief moments. You need a spot where you can relax, wind down, and gloat or despair (depending on your mood), ALONE. Other than the ideal office of your own, the best spot may be the school library. Here, you can usually find a quiet study carrel in the reference room. Another suggestion is your car. Or, you can take a walk outside. Sometimes, getting out of the building is its own best reward. For regular use, scout to see if an empty classroom is available in the building during your preparation periods. If so, find out if you may use it. Do not, however, barge in and occupy the room without asking first; you do not want to tread on someone else's territoriality by usurping their Hiding Space.

Your days will be busy and hectic. If you want to maintain the significance of your day, you will need a quiet corner, but find it BEFORE you are cornered.

Additional Space, or the I-Can-Do-It-All Syndrome

As a new teacher in school, you will be trying to prove your worth. In so doing, you may fall into the "Sure, I'll be happy to do it" response more often than will prove comfortable. Being overly accommodating, however, has no good reward; in fact, when doing our best becomes "overdoing," we can overextend ourselves into problematical situations.

You will be asked to do almost everything, perhaps even including sweeping the floors. One young teacher was asked to clean the floors of his room after school because the custodian was ill. Any surprising request is possible. Take them in stride!

Do what is asked of you as long as it's legal—check the union contract, if you have nagging suspicions. Looking for extra work, and even taking on extra work, is often tempting to the young teacher who thinks, "Yes, I'll show them that I can plan, teach, grade, fill out forms, coach the track team, advise the debate team, and sweep the floors, and take care of my family, all at the same time, while surviving my first year of teaching in one piece." Heroism is commendable, as long as it lasts, but when you go belly up, you'll look like a fool. You cannot be all things to all people all the time. Sooner or later, you'll crack, and your smiling, but tough, façade of willingness will give way to the perfectly ordinary human being inside who is neither godlike nor a machine.

If you take on any extra work, be sure you can complete it. Do not volunteer for extra duties on which you may not be able to follow through. **We advise:** Do what is expected of you according to the best of your ability. Do not bite off more than you can chew. If you find that you're having difficulty, speak to your supervisor. Do not hope that these things will just disappear. Confronting problems head-on and early will lead to solutions eventually.

Duty Space, or "Is This Why I Went to College?"

Very often, in the course of a school teacher's day, you will experience "the duty." The duty is time you spend monitoring students outside of your classroom. You may have a hall duty, a lunch duty, or a study-hall duty. You may have any combination of the above, depending on the school district in which you work.

If you find yourself sitting at an uncomfortable desk in the hallway checking student passes, do not despair. If you find yourself standing in the lunch room beside the steam table making sure that students do not cut into line, do not despair. Instead, be positive and look on the bright side! Study halls, lunch, and hall duties are all fine ways to meet with the students and the faculty on a different footing. Bring some work along, if that is allowed; if it isn't, bring some anyway, and do it surreptitiously. You will soon find that some of your most delightful encounters occur while you are on "duty."

Coming and Going Space

Be on time! Better: Be early!

We advise: Arrive at school at least one-half hour before you have to be there.

That quiet half-hour before the onrush is good private time for yourself. Few teachers and fewer students will be in school that early, and you will be able to get some preparation done, some last-minute photocopying, or some preview of the day's lessons. Moreover, you will earn the reputation for being a caring and diligent individual.

As ever, do not gloat over how early you get to school; keep that to yourself. Somebody at the top, nonetheless, may take note, and you will be rewarded both professionally and personally.

Most schools have union-okayed regulations about starting times and leaving times. Adhere to those times without question.

Do not be the first one out of your room; do not line up with the kids at the end of your last period; do not make a beeline for your car. After-school time is a good time to sit and reflect on the day's high-lights. After school is also a good time for appointments with parents, with students, or with your supervisor(s). If at all possible, plan on staying after school at least twenty to thirty minutes after the last bell has sounded. This is excellent time to prepare the next day's lessons, do your paperwork, and do some photocopying. Don't brag about your after-school time any more than you do about your before-school time. As ever: Speak softly, and do your own thing.

SICK DAYS

The school district did not hire a roboteacher; it hired a living, breathing human individual who occasionally gets sick, who has family members who occasionally get sick, and who has responsibilities outside of the school sphere. This is why sick days are built into union contracts.

Many new teachers carry around a low-grade fear that if they get ill and say so and take a day off, they will not be believed. They are fearful that they will be looked on with suspicion and mistrust upon their return. This fear is unfounded. In fact, coming in when you are contagious—coughing and feverish and spreading your germs around—can sometimes breed suspicion and anger.

People get sick. People need to rest when they are ill, and this is commonly understood. As a matter of fact, first-year teachers often get ill more often than previously because they are under a lot of new stress and because, not yet immune to the myriad school germs, they are exposed to all sorts of new diseases.

It was during Karen's first year of teaching that she became quite ill with a virus that would not go away. Believing herself to be a superwoman, Karen did not take off from school; rather, she came into work for a week with a terrible cold and a fever. At one point, she looked so bad that even her students told her to go home. Karen's supervisor called her into his office and informed her—quite angrily— that she had to go home, that she was endangering all those who came into contact with her, and that he would get a substitute for her that very minute. Being diligent and conscientious was turning out in Karen's case to be a liability to everyone concerned, Karen included.

FUTURE SPACE

While the physical design of your school is unlikely to change, one thing that can change is annual assignments. Your particular array of classes, rooms, and students will vary each year. At the point of change, you can open new opportunities for yourself. The difficulties with space you will probably have during your first year may find happy solutions in another school year. In the future, you can work towards getting the physical necessities of teaching arranged more to your liking. One of the best aspects of teaching is this constant renewal of self and setting—"future space."

Joan's department did not have enough classrooms for all the teachers to have their own rooms, though a few did. Each year, the chair struggled to reapportion the rooms fairly. Beyond everyone's wishes and wants, when a clear need could be demonstrated, it would tip the scale.

Joan happened to use many copied materials, and it was very difficult for her to carry her stacks of copies from place to place. Joan began decorating one of her rooms with students' displays, and she asked her chair to come view them. Towards the end of the year, Joan reminded the chair that she needed one classroom space to present all her students' work. She got her own room the next year.

One year, Michael shared a room with a teacher who was burned out. She happened to be teaching the same course as Michael. She left students' papers all over the desk and in the drawers. She lost homework papers continually. Michael overheard the end of each class when her lesson faded into nonsense; he watched her scurry from the class as if barely escaping with her life. Michael felt demoralized by her instability and by the daily necessity of having to clean up the mess after her—the cluttered desk and the chalkboard that she never erased—before his own class could begin.

So, Michael made a short-term plan to survive the year in the presence of this unhappy teacher. He moved her materials to one side of the desk and kept them there; he asked a student to erase the board, and another to open the windows each day. He consciously determined that, for the rest of the year, he would shape his class environment according to his own needs. He also decided that he would try to make sure that he would not be teaching in the same room as the burnt-out teacher in the coming year. Michael campaigned with his administrator for a different room on the basis of educational needs; he suggested that he share a room with a simpatico colleague with whom he could team-teach. The onerous situation of one year became an opportunity for positive change the next. Furthermore, Michael was praised for being an innovative teacher.

One aspect of the politics of space in your school is that it's bound to be the hardest and most opaque when it is all new. We have never known space realities NOT to be a problem for most teachers, whether they were old hands or greenhorns. If you can define what makes you uncomfortable in your teaching environment, then you can establish a plan to try to change it. You may not be able to change everything you want, but the best way to make school space work for you is by being realistic.

Rhythms

THE DAILY PATTERN AND THE YEARLY CYCLE

We school teachers know that the Hebrew calendar has it right: New Year's is in September, not in January. For the school-oriented, moreover, the year is only nine months long. The close of the year does not arrive on the last day of December, but on the final school day in June.

Unless a twelve-month school year has been adopted by your school, this fall-to-spring pattern will determine the rhythm of your teaching year. The school year, which originated in parallel with agricultural down-time, was invented to accommodate the seasons and farmer-parents' need for their children's labor in the fields. Now, however, the school year largely corresponds with our seasonal cycle: School vacations occur regularly in the autumn, the winter, the spring, and, of course, the long vacation of summer. This school/year cycle is, furthermore, imprinted deeply in our psyches from our earliest years. Once you become aware of the effects of alternating periods of anticipation and (get used to it!) lethargy, you can use the rhythmic cycle to increase your students' abilities to learn.

The rhythm of the school year has many phases and passages, many meters and beats, many colors and feels. Not only will the almost invisible clockwork of school time affect what happens within your classroom but also the ticking of the administrative year will have great impact both on how you are perceived within your school and how you feel yourself to be doing in your job.

Day by Day

Not only is there a yearly cycle to adjust to when you teach school but also each day has its own predictable pattern. The slow, sleepy early morning when it's difficult to "think" is followed by a productive time of concentration during the mid-morning. Elementary school teachers announce reading and math for this time slot. They know that the best work is done when the children are both awake and mentally present.

Excited distractibility is the norm near lunch-time. Following lunch, students start all over again with logy distractibility, and thereafter they descend into tired passivity towards the end of the school day. We've seen students seem exhausted in the last class of the day, yet five minutes after school, they are laughing and chattering energetically with their friends in the halls, and making headlong for playing fields. For many students, "real" life begins only after the school day is over.

Your life pulses to the same rhythms as your students' lives. When you are in the classroom, you will find you also experience the rhythms of the school day. The main difference between you and your students is that at the close of the day, you will not have the same amount of energy that they exhibit! While this beat goes on, one of your goals will be to make your students as active in the learning process as you are in the teaching mode. If your classes meet at the same time each school day, you will learn to take the rhythmic daily cycle into account by structuring your lessons to fit the constraints that each time slot places on the bodies, minds, and emotions of your students.

Establish a procedure that signals when class will begin. Yelling "Quiet!" over the noise is an ineffective way to start each class. Think ahead about the procedure you will use, build in a cost to the kids who don't follow it, and then be consistent. Establish the rhythm of the class at the very start, and stick to it!

Above all, have your materials organized so that they are at your fingertips, ready to go. The amount of paper and other materials that you will sort through each day does actually require the skills of an executive secretary to organize, so don't sneer at easy techniques that help you accomplish this task! Once you have spent the first hour of your first evening after your first day of real teaching, just separating your homework papers from your class notes from your copies of assignments from your administrative notices, you will begin to think highly of any trick that will help you organize all that paper.

Q IS FOR QUIET

School periods are relatively short; they were not designed for the completion of entire projects. If you have recently graduated from college or graduate school, you will have to readjust to the shorter and more intense rhythm of the shorter class periods in schools. The students are usually required to meet every class each day. Whether or not your school is moving to flexible scheduling, so that the periods vary in length or are rotated throughout the day, school days require tremendous stamina on your part and good coping mechanisms.

You will have the all-important preparation period to sit, rest, and enjoy the luxury of structuring your own time. Students, by contrast, cope by squeezing in as much social time with their friends as possible between class periods.

Give clear cues to your students about how your class formally will begin. You may decide to use the first five minutes for talk and organizing, but you must build in a cue—a downbeat (to keep our rhythm metaphor going)—so that the students will know when to become attentive to the material and to you. If the norm in your school is that all students are to be in the room or in their seats at the bell, then you must follow that rule. If the norm is that the students dash into the room after the bell, or even stroll into the room when they are ready, you won't be able to establish a different rule all by yourself. By being aware of school norms about the rhythms of the day, and following what already exists, you can build a positive atmosphere. A confrontation with a recalcitrant student at the start of class is a sure bet to ruin your well-planned lesson.

You want to begin each class by establishing a tone that will make you and your students comfortable. Consider using techniques like the following for getting your classes started with energy and purpose:

- Stand at the door before the period to greet students and also to make sure that they don't "hang around" in the halls and therefore enter your class late or "on the run."

- Provide "Do Nows" or five-minute projects that you place on the desks of the students just before they enter. Be sure to grade these "Do Nows" assiduously; make them quick and concrete, so you can return them at the next class meeting.

These organizing activities will be effective only if you give your students immedate feedback. Avoid using class time to correct these little activities, for you want to focus your students' attention on your all-class activities in order to teach something new.

- Consider taking attendance and giving penalties to those who do not quiet down at this cue.

- Require your students to open their notebooks by a specified time.

- Bang a gavel to bring your class to order.

- Use color-coded folders keyed to each class so you can easily locate specfic papers and materials. (We got this idea by watching our doctor's secretary organize her patients' folders.)

- Try weekly assignment sheets for your students, like the one on pp. 44-45. List the topics to be covered that week, and what the students must read, write, or practice; distribute this sheet once a week, and you will provide everyone with a new sense of purpose once a week. You will also short-circuit that endless, daily question: "What was the homework last night?" Assignment sheets also force you to keep up with the curriculum that you are supposed to cover, and they also serve as a basis for plan books, if your school requires written daily lesson plans.

- For yourself, keep track of all those assignments for all those classes for all those subjects for all those days by using a weekly assignment plan, like the one on pp. 46-47. "You can't tell the players without a program," and you can't maintain your own sanity without a daily and weekly plan.

Homework   Ms. Kramer
THROUGH AFRICAN EYES

"The main goal of *Through African Eyes* is to broaden our perspective by presenting a largely African view of Africa and the world."

Leon Clark
Preface, *Through African Eyes*

Monday, Oct. 7

Re-work your list of family members into an anthropological family tree. Due next Monday.

Bring *Through African Eyes* to class tomorrow and for the rest of the week.

Tuesday, Oct. 8

1. What inaccuracies can you find in the Nacirema article? (at least 3)

2. Explain how or why the anthropologist might have made this mistake.

3. Try to define the following three terms: perception, misperception, preconditioning

Wednesday, Oct. 9

Complete your sheets on the Bushmen tape.

Thursday, Oct. 10

Write a "piece" which is any of the following: an experience, the plot of a movie you've seen, the plot of a book you've read, a story you have heard about, or a fictionalized account of an event in which the following ideas or concepts came into play.

racial superiority	images of other groups	stereotype
self-image	prejudice	empathy

Your "piece" may be a first draft. However, your account requires a heading, margins, neat handwriting (typing preferred) and real organization. The above words need to be used in the unfolding of your "piece."

Homework   Ms. Kramer
THROUGH AFRICAN EYES (continued)

Friday, Oct. 11

Please read over your sheets on "The Memories of Your Friends and Parents."

Pick one of the "Historical Memories" at the end that you find interesting or true.

Find from one to four examples within the document which prove the truth of the idea you picked.

Write one to three paragraphs presenting the memory and "proving" it with the examples you found in the document.

You will have to "quote" from my quotes.

Do not say "I" in this paper.

Do not use "he" or "she" in this paper.

Use all the rules for writing that you have learned thus far.

ASSIGNMENT SHEET

WEEK: 2/1-2/9/93

CLASS	For TUESDAY 2/2 #7	For WEDNESDAY 2/3 #8	For THURSDAY 2/4 #1
E 3 S	FINAL DISCUSSIONS: FRANKENSTEIN RESPONSE: DISCUSS THE IRONY OF VICTOR'S NAME —	RESPONSE: DISCUSS FRANKENSTEIN AS A ROMANTIC NOVEL.	NO CLASS ←——→
E 3 M	LITERATURE TEXT P. 346, "EPIGRAMS" P. 347 — QUESTIONS #1-6	P. 354, "EPIGRAMS" P. 356 — QUESTIONS #1-5	① P. 341, POEM P. 341, QUESTIONS ② P. 351, POEM P. 352, QUESTIONS
E 2 H	VOCAB: TEST PP. 135-149 LITERATURE TEXT: → WHITMAN "SONG OF MYSELF" → QUESTIONS	WHITMAN → WHEN... ASTRONOMER THIS DUST... MAN NOISELESS... SPIDER NOW LIFT ME CLOSE → QUESTIONS	DICKENSON GROUPS TO → → →
I C	LITERATURE TEXT: READ "BEAT, BEAT DRUM" P. 274 P. 275, ALL QUESTIONS	READ P. 287 - "THE BUSTLE IN A HOUSE" QUESTIONS, P. 289 # 1, 2, 3	RESPONSE: WHAT POEM DO YOU LIKE BEST? WHY?

ASSIGNMENT SHEET (continued)

For Friday 2/5 #2	For Monday 2/8 #3	For Tuesday 2/9 #4	Notes
TEST: FRANKENSTEIN	THESIS STATEMENT DUE ESSAY - FRANKENSTEIN ↘ DUE TODAY → TYPED → DOUBLE-SPACED → COVER SHEET	↘ BEGIN COOP. UNIT HW — → POEMS, P. 483, P. 484 P. 484 - QUESTIONS	
→ REVIEW GAME: PREPARE 10 SHORT ANSWER QUESTIONS + 2 ESSAYS → PROVIDE ANSWERS!	No CLASS ←——→	VOCAB: → UNIT 10 → GLOSSARY → EXERCISES, PP. 97-101	FOR WED. TEST 17TH & 18TH CENTURIES
ASSIGN HOMEWORK → → → → ALL POEMS TO BE FINISHED TODAY	THESIS STATEMENT DUE DICKENSON OVERFLOW DAY	WHITMAN OVERFLOW DAY	WED TEST WHITMAN DICKENSON
FINISH READING "TO BUILD A FIRE" ↘ QUESTIONS, P. 345, 1-6	VOCAB: → UNIT 10 → GLOSSARY → EXERCISES, PP. 97-101	LITERATURE TEXT FOR A REVIEW GAME: → PREPARE 10 SHORT ANSWER QUESTIONS → PREPARE 2 ESSAYS → WRITE ANSWERS!	FOR WED. TEST 19TH CENTURY

Occasionally, you may take a ribbing from others for being "too" organized. We've seen colored paper clips to match color-coded folders, teachers pushing hand-carts filled with their students' work, and teachers carrying two briefcases cram-packed with paper plus whatever else they had under their arms. Better to be "too" organized, however, than to face a roomful of kids without a clue as to what to do next! Watch how the best-organized teachers in your school store their materials. Ask for concrete advice on this issue. Every teacher is proud of the tricks of the trade that years of practice have honed.

How and when should you end your classes? In elementary schools, classes and subjects tend to overlap one another such that the flow of the day feels more whole. Secondary schools allow a minimal amount of time between classes for students to pass from one room to another. While you chat with students, clean up materials, and prepare for your next class, your students will be streaming into the halls to socialize between classes. You may have to erase the board, re-wind a film, pack away homework, file materials, and move to another room for your next class. How can you handle these crucial few minutes so that you remain calm, cool, and collected at the start of each class in your day?

Learn to do formal closure with each class. It gives you and your students alike a feeling of having finished, hence preparing you for what comes next. To close your classes formally, you need to be the one who watches the clock. Close your class surely and well at least a couple of minutes before the bell. If you do, that infamous last-minute bluster and hurry that confuses students and puts teachers out of control will disappear.

Announce that you cannot entertain long questions between classes. The end of class is also not the time for shouting out the next day's assignment. (Your weekly assignment sheet is intended to take care of that task.) After you announce the end of class, your students will be pressed to pack up their books, see their friends, occasionally ask you brief questions, and then get to their next class on time. If you are calm and organized, the rhythm of your classes will be calm and organized too.

THE PULSE OF THE YEAR

At the same time, the lock-step rigidity of the school day is criss-crossed by the flow of the school year. As a beginning teacher, you can learn to cope with the constraints of school time and capitalize upon the seasons of the school year by being observant of your own and your students' needs, and by helping yourself and them to accommodate to the rhythms of school life. You can reshape school time to your own advantage.

The Back-to-School Honeymoon Period (Late August, September, and October)

The fall of the year! Cooler days and invigorating weather! Harvest time and autumn leaves! Labor Day signals the beginning of a new year of work and new opportunities for a fresh start, not only at school but also throughout all of society, as the pace of life seems to pick up. Advertisers pitch pictures at us of new fall clothes in sun-dappled playing fields filled with autumnal colors of gold, yellow, purple, red, and brown. Magazines and TV ads display students full of purpose, even holding books. We all get another new chance in September, and teachers and students alike resolve to make this new year a new beginning.

The new energy and hopefulness define a honeymoon period for both you and your students, an era of good feelings when students, teachers, and administrators alike are all on their best behavior.

Take advantage of the opportunity that this willingness to co-operate engenders. Although you may have difficulty sleeping the night before your first day of classes, and you may obsessively plan every word of what you will try to teach that first day, you can relax. You really don't succeed or fail based on what happens on Day One.

Adolescents will see your classroom differently from the way you see it. They are alert to social opportunities for proving themselves and maintaining their social positions. Most of your students will be concentrating on each other, and the emphasis will be social, not academic. Plan some structured socializing time into your first class activities so that everyone can get to know each other. You want to get to know their names quickly to establish personal relationships with each student and the control that this acquaintance gives you.

English teachers often begin class during the first week with a journal or a series of writing assignments in which they try to elicit information about the personalities of their students. Other teachers play name games in schools where the students in each class are not likely to know everyone else. Having the students interview one another, and then having the interviewer introduce the interviewee to the class, is a good way to get to know everyone. Try a student questionnaire or survey in which you ask important questions, such as what they learned in the subject during the previous year, or who their friends are in the class, or what school experience has made them feel the best about themselves.

Build opportunities into your class activities to acknowledge the individual personalities of your students. About the end of October (the usual end of the honeymoon period) you might institute a new policy of changing every student's seat about every two or three weeks. Occasional changes in the social mix allow you to get to know your students better, and the changes force them to get to know one another better. Freely move students away from others with whom they clash or with whom they cannot keep from talking.

Make your moves quietly before class starts. Require that objections to your moves and policies be discussed with you in privacy after class. Try to keep class-time on track for academic work, while encouraging students nonetheless to talk with you about other issues outside of class.

You might develop a seating rotation plan that takes effect after each major examination. In your rotation make sure that the next-seat neighbors are always different people. When your students grumble, laugh, and call it the volleyball rotation! Pull the students from the back rows down to the front, and move the people who have profited by being at the front, back to the back. Shake things up, and you'll be leveling the playing field, smoothing out the social wrinkles. The right kind of change can help reinstitute that honeymoon feeling, and it keeps you in control, as well.

MRS. KRAMER—

I DISCOVERED THAT IT MAKES A WORLD OF DIFFERENCE TO SIT IN THE FRONT OF CLASS. IN THE BACK, IT IS EASY TO SLEEP, LOOK OUT THE WINDOW, ETC. FROM THE FRONT OF THE CLASS, IT IS MUCH MORE EXCITING. I AM NOT BORED, AND AM INTERESTED IN THE CURRICULUM. I JUST WANTED YOU TO KNOW THAT I USED TO HATE YOUR ROTATING CLASS, AS WELL AS YOUR ROTATING SEAT SYSTEM. NOW I THINK IT'S GREAT!

—HT

P.S.—IT WOULD BENIFIT ME GREATLY TO SIT IN FRONT OF THE ROOM. PLEASE TRY TO KEEP THIS IN MIND.

—THANK YOU

PLEASE GIVE ME A RESPONSE NOTE IF YOU WISH.

When you can connect every name on your roster with every face in front of you, and when you see that all your students are not learning in quite the way you imagined they would, the honeymoon may be over, but your best working period is about to begin.

Neophyte teachers are usually warned that what happens in September will lock them into patterns for the entire school year. If you remain passive before the juggernaut of school time, then that may happen to you; on the contrary, however, we have found that you can modify the patterns all year by observing the rhythms. The beat goes on, but you can call the tune.

Your students will want to know up front how difficult your course is going to be, and how much work they will have to do. They can be so delicate with their inquiries: "Will this course be as boring as they say it was last year?"

Although it is tempting, at first, to want to explain that your course will be unique or different from all their previous courses, if you promise more than you can deliver, your students will remember your "false advertising" until the last day of June. You might, therefore, want to take a wait-and-see attitude. Be sure that you can deliver what you promise. Build in a little mystery about yourself and about the course: You will also be building interest, while allowing yourself some leeway to develop your own patterns gradually.

The outer limits of behavior that you allow in September and the minimum standard for academics in October are what you will be tied to after the autumn honeymoon period is past. Although you can adjust specific operating rules, be sure to establish your outermost limits exactly where you want them. Smile and be friendly, but maintain your behavior and performance standards with noble exactitude. Be consistent. Be clear. Formal presentations, clear-cut directions, and high-minded but reasonable expectations will build cooperative behavior.

Autumn honeymoon or not, all those mundane rules about who may go to the bathroom when and under what conditions, policy on late homework, how to make up missed tests, and all the rest ought to be clearly set out right away. You may not have to state these rules in writing, but you will want to put them into practice immediately.

We advise: New teacher, be realistic! As an idealistic new teacher, you will be tempted to establish rules that would fit only the best of all possible teaching worlds. If you don't know the norms of your school yet, be circumspect in laying down laws that you might not be able to enforce. Rule-making in new situations is always very difficult. If you can possibly ask several teachers in your school what policies they follow, you might discover what practice in your school is acceptable and comfortable. Or you may lean towards scrapping the ideal of establishing clear rules in favor of deciding how to proceed on a case-by-case, situation-by-situation basis. Whichever way you go as a new teacher, your best chance for reasonable rules is to proceed as lightly as possible while you are still exploring your expectations and establishing your own rhythms.

The Period of "Class Struggle"

Some, even many, of your students will probably have done poorly on your first test. This defeat shatters the warm feelings that were generated during those first few days of back-to-school infatuation. The honeymoon is over; the marriage has begun. Now, you and your class begin the process of finding more realistic approaches that will work for you both. This second stage of the school year we call "the period of class struggle." The days grow shorter, the light weaker, and long winter seems to set in early. With the holiday season far ahead and offering only temporary respite, the period of class struggle will last until some time in the early spring.

C IS FOR CLASS STRUGGLE

The period of class struggle is typified by several challenging situations. This is the passage during which mistakes, miscalculations, failed lessons, sagging interest, and temper tantrums arising from both you and your students, cloud the atmosphere like blizzards and ice storms. This is a necessary process that enables you and them to come to know each other; it is also an unavoidable stage in any group process of serious and effective working together. Ameliorate the rigors of this inevitable stage by acknowledging it, understanding it, and congratulating yourselves on all your successes as you work your way through it, step by step.

Your students will pressure you to lower your expectations of what they can do, the level at which you teach, and your demand that they learn new study skills. If you present a new style of assignment or project, they may argue that they can't possibly do this project because they already have one in another course.

Their objections may or may not be true. Some wonderful schools set aside special days or weeks for each subject area to test or to assign research projects. If your school does not do this, you might use the information from your "first-week questionnaire" to ask your students' other teachers what major projects they are planning. With this knowledge, you can announce your own special efforts with the least possible conflict.

When you announce an upcoming test, students may alternately beg and demand a postponement. Completing every class activity may seem to take several more days than you planned. When this happens, simplify your lessons so that you use a portion of the period to introduce and explain basic terms or vocabulary that the students need to understand or discuss your topic. Design your lessons for quick feedback, for example, an announced two-question quiz that immediately follows your explanations or their note-taking. In other words, if you are feeling that you are losing their attention, pull them back by restructuring your lessons.

Even when you may have been perfectly clear and perfectly fair, you will still be confronted by minor rebellions in your classes during this period of the year when the days grow short and your students handle academic stress by resisting work and testing you. The period of class struggle is further typified by great swings in class performance. Some days, everything will click, and you will leave school feeling like the great teacher you know you can be. Other days will fill you with frustration and feelings of failure.

Another battle that takes place during the class struggle is over grades. A fine line runs between the discussion of a student's work regarding ways to improve it, and a debate about the appropriateness of a student's grade. Grading policy is a part of the class struggle that you will need to work out in order to be truly fair to yourself and your students. Whether you decide to be a tough grader going strictly by a number average, or a flexible grader using improvement and effort variables, explain your system and use it consistently.

Grading periods or marking terms are part of the rhythmic beat in the school year. Whether you have three or four terms, or more, these periods also mark intermediate beginnings and ends. Notify your students at the beginning of the term whether you are willing to allow any make-up or extra-credit work. Write out a policy statement that you think is fair, and stand by it. Some students will probably complain that they have had too few tests and quizzes to have a fair chance at what they consider to be a good grade, whereas others will moan that you have over-tested them. Plan to have three or four major grades and several smaller ones each marking term. Major grades do not always have to be hour-long tests; they can also be papers, projects, talks, and organizational work in groups. You can teach your students that the processes they use are as important as the results they achieve by grading their process performance as well as the outcome.

One way to be victorious in the class struggle so that it becomes a win/win situation for all is by being aggressively innovative. New types of projects and novel assignments often reawaken new enthusiasm among the students during the winter doldrums. For example, without removing the onus of no-credit for poor or incomplete academic work, offer extra-credit projects that integrate aesthetic expression with academic work. Stimulate your students to initiate their own ideas for new projects. Plan for some cooperative groups and active projects in which strong students might assist weaker ones. Set up peer-teaching duos, or have mini-contests between learning teams during reviews for tests. Once you know the skills and personalities of your students, you can organize teams that work well.

Little notes of congratulation or comments of praise for a good comment in class can help your students feel satisfied about their work. Even using "happy faces" can encourage a discouraged student to keep trying. Borrow the school photography equipment, or use your own camera to take photos of your students at work, and then post your shots on the bulletin board. Vanity is great when it is combined with academic achievement. Indications of appreciation, whether large or small, can mitigate the traumas of the winter blahs.

The great advantage of knowing about the struggles of this stage of the school year is that you can avoid the doubt that often accompanies the onset. Your students' reactions are not necessarily based on your presumptive failure to have motivated them. If you are ready to accept these variations as normal both in your professional development and in the unfolding rhythms of the school year, you can laugh at the bad days and take heart at the progress you make on the good ones.

Use the wintertime class struggle to your advantage. First, acknowledge to your students that you are aware that it is a hard time of the year, and that you are also aware that they are working hard. Accept the responsibility for explaining to your students why your subject is worth your teaching and their learning. Now is your opportunity to teach your students what real academic work is all about.

You place value on what you are doing—tell your students so. Explain how you got interested in your subject and why it is still alive for you. Explain why learning requires real work. Assure them that the work is worthwhile. Extend yourself in honest and forthright appreciation for the work that they accomplish.

Take every opportunity to help your students feel successful. Find opportunities to give second chances for the students who haven't done well. After all, although school is a preparation for the real world of the workplace or for college, school is not the same as adulthood, and the same make-it-or-break-it rules need not apply. Education requires the flexibility and the opportunity to re-educate when your students fail to learn. You may be teaching reading, writing, and 'rithmetic, but you are also teaching the skills of negotiation, good manners, and civility. Demonstrate—"model" (as we teachers like to say)—those skills in your management of your students, and you will be teaching them the humane behaviors that will make of them responsible, civilized citizens and worthwhile human beings.

Acknowledge the period of struggle by assuring students that you do know when an assignment is especially difficult or time-consuming. Occasionally extend a deadline when you can see that the stress is too great. Students are like other people: They need to feel that they are in control of their situations; they need to feel that that they may learn from their mistakes, rather than that they will be punished for them.

Another ongoing reality in the era of class struggle is that the students are working out their social relationships with each other. Personal dislikes and rivalries among your students can take on serious proportions with disruptive effects for your teaching and learning agenda. Students often use their time in class to make points with their friends and secure their places within their peer groups. If you are oblivious to this sub-text being played out in your classroom, you'll struggle much harder than you need to. Learn to see and know, where you need to; learn to be blind and deaf, where it is useful.

In one corner of Larissa's class of thirty students, this new teacher observed that the atmosphere seemed different from the rest of the class. In that part of the room, comments were freely offered, and banter was common during each lesson. An intimacy existed among these students in which socializing and commenting took precedence over any other activity. Larissa tried frequent seat changes to stop the personal exchanges, but she never got over the feeling that the class was acting out a sub-text of student interaction quite apart from the academic play. Larissa discussed it with other teachers and even with her class, laughed about it and chastised the students individually, but the proximity of friends and the need to show off was inextinguishable. Larissa learned, within limits, to let it be.

You can use the social whirl to your advantage in the classroom, just as you can use the class-struggle period of the school year, if you remain flexible and adaptable. Look for opportunities to introduce variety and prompt change, and hang on tight: Help is coming. (They don't put winter vacation in there for nothing! The Big Change from the old year to the new, and the novelty of the holidays, is the life raft that many teachers and students alike ride to safety in order to escape the winter doldrums.)

Be good to yourself, and be good to your students. Reward yourself and your students for any good work that you both do. Find occasions for humor and individual rewards. Change-of-pace lessons, such as a French Revolution Party in which everyone dresses up with tri-colors and Marie Antoinette's wig, plays a character, and brings in French food such as brie cheese and red-white-and-blue cake inscribed "Let them eat cake," can perk up a winter class. Or plan a game-day in which you play "Jeopardy" with questions and answers from your academic material. Give prizes! Be innovative! Re-invigorate your classes with controlled craziness!

The Holidays

The school year is punctuated by several important beginnings and endings. Vacations require planning because they involve a temporary parting. Many students find this upsetting; their anticipation of vacation time can interfere with their abilities to work or to cooperate with you and with each other.

Pre-planning can alleviate these tensions and redirect students' energies into positive learning experiences. For instance, plan an unusual class activity, such as a trial or contest or play, that makes the last week before holidays both fun and different, yet requires some analytical work such as writing or a test. Tests, even on the last day, are also a good idea for keeping the work-level high. Some teachers use the final day before vacations to show slides of their own vacations to exotic places or to have some type of new activity.

Don't get caught unprepared before a vacation. Close the class carefully. Do not extend tests or projects over a holiday vacation. Don't necessarily send them home with a lot of homework to do during their holidays. Give yourself and your students a chance to rest and regenerate.

Best of all, holidays provide opportunities for new resolutions and fresh starts. When you return from vacation, rested, relaxed, and ready for another go at schooling, you and your students will enjoy a mini-honeymoon period. With this new beginning, you and they can restructure what you remember that you didn't like before the holidays.

Spring: The Teacher's Harvest

Springtime is both a danger and a great challenge. Academic momentum begins to sag as spring fever becomes epidemic, and the returning light and warm afternoons promise the fun of outdoors, vacation, and summertime.

You are called upon to maintain consistency of discipline and application in order to keep the work of learning going forward. If you are building towards the grand climax of a final exam, you need to assure your students that you are in charge and that you will be able to prepare them for the test. Be sure to allow plenty of time for a fair review period, even if you have to stop short in your teaching. Last minute work crammed into too short a time-period will not help your students learn, and it will make them resent you.

Springtime, the final period of the year, is all too brief, but it can be very sweet. In this stage, you and your students know each other's foibles and have even come to accept them.

It was in springtime when Jennifer's students groused lightheartedly about her almost daily hand-outs of photocopied materials from newspapers, books, and magazines. They lamented mightily, groaning that she would be known to posterity as a "tree-killer." When her school began an environmental program and collected used paper, she called herself a "rapid recycler."

On the other hand, springtime can threaten failure both for you and your students. Carl, a frustrated new teacher confronted by an intractable student, used a business technique to help himself and the student survive through to the end of the school year. Carl transformed his role from stern punisher to an understanding mentor.

The student had established a pattern of coming late every day to class, arriving with no notebook but with a sour and defeatist attitude. Carl was feeling angrier and angrier as each fruitless day passed by. One spring day, the inevitable happened. Carl's unhappy student exploded into the classroom long after the late bell. The other students laughed, waiting for the expected confrontation between teacher and student. But this teacher knew by now that his student desperately needed to pass this course in order to graduate in June.

Carl calmly walked over to his recalcitrant pupil, and he whispered: "See me after class." The student, expecting a stern rebuke, found that his teacher had something else in mind. Carl offered his nemesis a deal.

"Is it important for you to graduate in June?" Carl asked.

"Yes," the disarmed student replied.

"Then I've got an idea that might work for us both. Let's write a contract just between us. It will be strictly private—nobody else will know about it or its terms. It will specify what you have to do to get a passing grade, and if you do what you contract with me to do, I guarantee that you will pass. Deal?"

"You'll guarantee me a passing grade?" The student was shocked.

"You follow through on whatever terms we negotiate, and you will have earned your grade," replied Carl.

From that time onward, the relationship between student and teacher became much less confrontational. Although Carl privately had to remind his student once or twice when he failed to fulfill one term or another of the contract, the businesslike approach secured a truce and paid off in a handsome dividend at the end of the year for them both. The kid graduated, and Carl knew that his first year of teaching had been a success.

Here is an actual "school contract" that one of us used with one of our students:

May 1, 1990

CONTRACT BETWEEN JEREMY BILGRE AND MRS. KRAMER

Jeremy agrees to do the following until the Regents Exam.

1. Come to class on time, take seat and open notebook.
2. No talking or communicating with other students during classtime.
3. Complete all classwork as requested by teacher.
4. Complete the paper on the Industrial Revolution.

In exchange, Mrs. Kramer promises to:

1. Keep the 10 points added to Jeremy's average for third term.
2. Guarantee a C or better for the fourth term.
3. Make every effort to make sure Jeremy passes this course and passes the Regents.

_____

Jeremy Bilgre

_____

Mrs. Kramer

The end of school threatens final grades. Be sure to place the emphasis in your grading where you think it should be. Students will often try to get you to change grades. But the first June afternoon that you overhear an undeserving student run from your class boasting ecstatically, "I got the teacher to give me that B-!" is a most chilling experience, and it will awaken you far more soberly than any advice we could give about the perverse willingness of some students to manipulate a teacher.

If you end your teaching year with the same reliable energy and organization that has been your habitual rhythm throughout all the seasons, your students will reward you with a pleasant spring. Your own awareness of this final denouement in the rhythmic nature of a school-year course of study enables you to minimize conflicts and increase learning.

In this stage of the year, many students make an academic and social leap. They appear already to be members of the next grade; they seem to be older, more tolerant, brighter, and nicer. They are, indeed, older, and also by now you have learned to compensate for their weaknesses, to avoid their vulnerable spots, and to reward them for their growth. Most of them will have learned to do the same for you. They are now employing all the terms and methods you have taught them; now you can reap the harvest that you have worked so hard to sow throughout the school year.

Spring, Tenure, and You

While you are busily doing everything you can to help your students negotiate the academic shoals of springtime, your administrators may be planning to sink you. Administrators finalize decisions about keeping their staff on the basis of student schedules for the following year. If they don't work out, you don't luck out.

The jobs of non-tenured teachers are always vulnerable in the spring of the school-year. Drops in student enrollment, or competition between departments for money and staff, can put positions in jeopardy. Non-tenured teachers have few legal rights of job protection. No matter how good you are, you may not be rehired.

Amy had been brought up in the Horatio Alger mode of American work ethic. Her parents encouraged her to believe that if she worked hard, she would do a good job, and if she did a good job, she would be recognized and rewarded by her employer. When Amy started teaching, she enthusiastically spent afternoons and weekends developing materials and attending workshops. She designed imaginative courses for her students. She received fine evaluations both fall and spring. Then, despite it all, she was told in April that her job was going to disappear because of low student enrollment. Amy couldn't help thinking both that she had been tricked and that she had failed, although neither of her emotional reactions was an accurate reflection of the situation.

No one had told Amy about the realities of employment and evaluations in schools. If your job is under threat in any way, go ahead and apply for positions elsewhere. After half the school year is complete, inquire of your supervisor often about your position for next year. You must protect yourself first; don't naively expect the school administration to take care of you. Ignore the advice of colleagues who will reassure you that "somehow things always work out for the best." The fact is that things may work out horridly for you. If your job is not guaranteed, you must look elsewhere.

. . . and the Beat Goes On: Summer Vacation

One of the favorite parts of Joe's school year is the summer. During the winter, he collects notices of workshops, courses, and project ideas in his subject field. To him, one advantage of secondary-school teaching is returning to the university in the summer to take courses. He finds them refreshing. He says that other teachers who attend these courses are interesting and fun to be with. This is his renewal. He returns to the classroom in September with new lessons, interesting readings, and rejuvenated enthusiasm. For Joe, the summer is a time of renewal of academic learning and professional commitment.

Joe's colleague, Paul, however, takes his family on extended camping trips during the long vacation. Paul wants a break from reading and academic work; he wants to see new places. Other teachers work on hobbies, take second jobs, or curl up with a good book. Paul wants a long rest.

Summer is the period of the school year guilty of promoting the notion among those who are DEFINITELY not in the know that teaching is a lark. Most of us who chose teaching with noble aspirations in mind also believed the myth: "Go into teaching; the pay is low, but at least you have two months off in the summer." We have all been told at one time or another, "Either get a real job or stop complaining; after all, you do have so-o-o-o-o much vacation time." What can our rebuttal be?

The fact is that summer is an integral component of the teacher's rhythmic year. Regardless of what the public illusion is—or should we say "delusion"—summer must be considered to be a part of the school year, not apart from the year. A mentor of ours once stated that summertime is the root that supplies the energy necessary to begin the teaching cycle again.

The sharp teacher is the teacher who harnesses energy, rather than burning it. Every season of the school year requires thought and planning. The lyric, "Summertime and the living is easy," does not preclude your working. Even if you need to work a second job during the summer, the change of pace can be a relief. Successful teaching is an intellectual and creative process that does not stop in July and August. Notice that we say "successful teaching" as opposed to "teaching." One of your goals in learning the profession is to learn to make the summers work for you. Understanding that the summer is an opportunity for renewal and invigoration is a step along the road to success.

We believe that the successful teacher is the teacher who attends classes, who is continually on the alert for new ideas, new methods, and new solutions. We also believe that the burnout often associated with the teaching profession is due to the grinding regularity of the rhythm in the school year. Rejoice in your summer, and avoid burnout!

Summertime is your time for yourself; if you can share with your colleagues what you have learned, then that is a bonus, but it is not essential. During summer vacation, enrich yourself for yourself, and for the sake of enriching your students also. You should be able to return to school in the fall with the very same feeling of expectation and excitement that your students feel, raring to go.

V IS FOR VACATION

SYSTEMS

When you walk through the door of your school, you enter a labyrinth of interconnected mazes of personal, professional, administrative, and—above all—political connections (and disconnections), that will require every ounce of savvy you can muster to negotiate. You will probably never fathom all the ins and outs of the Byzantine goings-on in your school that mean either life or death for you as a teacher, but be aware that you are now a part of these complicated relationships and struggles taking place in your school.

THE HUM OF THE SYSTEM

As assuredly as the school year has its rhythms, so also the school system has its hum. In much the same way as the rhythms of your classroom run either in sync with, or at counterpoint to, the rhythms of the rest of the school, so also are other sections of the educational orchestra beating out their own time, playing their own tunes. The percussion of administration regulates the pace at which everyone else marches, but those drums and gongs and whistles go off at times quite on their own, quite without regard for what anyone else is doing. The brass of school politics is sometimes loud and sometimes mellow, but you can always hear it playing. And then, there's the little piccolo— you, the new teacher—tootling along, being listened to, and evaluated, by everyone, both officially and unofficially.

THE POLITIC RHYTHM OF COLLEGIALITY

Louise once had a business consultant from outside of the school working with her in an economics course. The consultant had worked in a medium-sized business for thirty years. After retirement, she volunteered to assist high-school teachers. Upon entering the faculty room of the school, she exclaimed, "I can't believe this. It's so small. Where are your desks? How can you work like this?"

The regulars in the room were, nevertheless, perfectly comfortable sitting around overcrowded tables. They often got great amounts of work done, but—more importantly—they used preparation periods to tease, gossip, debate world cultural and political events, and in numerous ways to encourage each other.

Groups of teachers form complex social networks. Teachers new to the school need to take plenty of time to observe how these relationships affect teaching. It is often difficult for young teachers, in particular, to wend their ways through the complexities of relationships with people many years older, and many-school-years more experienced, than they are.

Teachers can become hearty colleagues, and even lasting friends, but they must be, at least, professional peers. The high opinion of your colleagues will make you feel at home and appreciated, but you must earn that high opinion. Let their good opinion of you develop over time—don't either demand or expect it at first. The most you can expect is your colleagues' judicious wait-and-see attitude. The rhythm of building solid relationships with your fellow teachers must of necessity be slow. New teachers come and go every year! Be friendly, be professional, and make observation your forte for at least a year.

MARCHING TO THE BEAT OF THEIR OWN DRUM:
The School Administration

Even as you focus on your daily round of lessons and the joys and travails of interacting with students, you must be aware of that whole greater reality swirling about and above you—the administration. It is no mere accident of history that our modern educational structure is a direct descendant of the medieval university. Just as you are like a feudal lord in the manor of your own classroom, where you set the laws, distribute justice, oversee work, and grant largesse in the form of grades and favors, so also are you a vassal in the feudal system above you. You owe your loyalty to this system and its overlords, and it in return provides your living and your protection.

In the Middle Ages, and still today, neophyte university teachers depended on their apprenticeship to powerful, experienced masters who mentored them along the upward path to full professorships. You, similarly, are dependent upon the political good will of your immediate superior, usually a chairperson, but sometimes a departmental committee, or a member of the higher administrative elite. Your immediate supervisor will be in charge of your future. The mystery of who rehires you often stumps new teachers. Is it your chair? The principal? The school board? In most schools, your direct administrative supervisor is the one who decides your future. The entire school bureaucracy only rubber-stamps this decision.

Who becomes an administrator? The best teachers often do not, although some do. Administrators wield a different kind of power than teachers do, they make bigger salaries, and usually they do not actively teach anymore. They are managers and overseers, and their roles compare much more closely with the business world of management than with the world of the teacher's classroom. Even when administrators do still teach classes, their other role removes them from the typical concerns of teachers.

Taking a problem to an administrator is a bit like presenting a case to the Supreme Court. You may feel that your troubled students need a higher authority than yourself to make decisions about their behavior, but the administrator may refuse to hear your case, especially if the case you are presenting is one that the administrator cannot confidently decide.

As in all other matters, most schools establish unwritten, customary policies regarding disciplinary procedures. Only when you have acquired sufficient knowledge about how your administrators deal with kids' problems, can you then decide how and when to bring the pressing problems to the people in authority.

Administrators also vary in terms of how they respond to parental pressure. In some schools, a call to an administrator by an upset parent will evoke an immediate and helpful response, and the administrator will mediate between you and the parent. A good administrator will not call you on the carpet over something that a parent has said about your class, but a not-so-good-one might.

If your administrator upbraids you for something that a parent alleges that you have done, behave professionally, keep your cool, and be honest. Even as adults, we teachers sometimes register a childish response to the administrators above us in whom the system invests great authority. If you feel intimidated by an administrator's behavior, don't show it. Calmly ask for an explanation of the problem at hand. Inquire why you are being asked any questions. Act with professional dignity, and require that the administrator behave likewise and treat you with collegiality.

If you have been caught off-guard, it is always permissible to say that you are pressed for time, and to arrange another appointment for another day. Take the time to think through the situation and what you want to say. A new teacher in a tight spot with an angry parent, a tough kid, and an unhelpful and harried administrator, is very vulnerable.

Respect your administrators, but do not give them more authority than they are due. During the final examination in June, Jo-ann was instructed via an administrative memo that no one was to be given permission to leave the classroom during the exam period. Towards the end of the exam, Jo-ann's punk student called her over and, with a dazed expression, told her that he had to go eat an apple. Jo-ann was surprised, and she assumed that he had taken some sort of drug.

Even though she could see that something was dreadfully wrong, Jo-ann followed school procedure and—per administrative memo—refused to let the student leave the room. After the exam was over, when the student was in a state of near-collapse, however, Jo-ann rushed to the phone to call the nurse, the boy's parents, and the school drug counselor. In the nurse's office, the unhappy student was able to ingest some sugar in time for his system to regain its equilibrium. The student's mother explained that her son was too proud and embarrassed to mention to the teacher that he was having a diabetic attack. Administrators are not gods; neither are their pronouncements inspired scripture. You are the highest authority in your classroom; use your own good sense to make necessary decisions!

Administrators We Have Known

School administrators can deceive you by their manners. Although many of them can be quite supportive, others can mislead you with false appearances:

❖ *The Administrative Wolf-in-Sheep's-Clothing:* This type encourages you, at first meeting, but then does nothing to help you during your first year.

❖ *The Administrative Manipulator:* This is the bureaucrat who keeps you on pins and needles about the possibilites of being rehired for next year.

❖ *The Administrative Mentor Waiting for a Protégé:* Not so friendly as it seems, this one is really your competitor, someone wanting to prove to self and others that his or her teaching is superior to yours.

Each of these species has been reported to be active in private and public schools of all kinds. Schools are no different from the rest of the work world. Pair your high aspirations with a sober attitude based on your eyes-open awareness of the realities of human nature. Even if your goal is the admirable and classic dream to be a wonderful teacher for whom school politics is sublimely irrelevant, there's no point in being so naive that you undermine your own hopes for success.

A romantic view of school administrators ill-prepares us for dealing on a professional level with the realities of school administrative bureaucracies. Administrators are human beings with all the mixture of good and evil, talent and dullness, ability and ineptitude that being human brings with it. If you rely unrealistically on your adminstrator—trying to make him or her into something that she or he is not—you have no one to blame but yourself.

When Rodney went to work at his first job in public-school teaching, he expected his administrative chair to treat him with almost the same TLC that his supervising teacher had used when Bob was doing his student teaching. He thought he could pour out his problems, and the administrator would make helpful suggestions for handling troublesome students and for structuring lessons more effectively.

Rodney was horrified, therefore, when he discovered that the chair was annoyed by his beginner's questions. The administrator, instead of being helpful, gave advice that turned into elusive dead-ends. Requests for materials were greeted with orders to check the departmental book closet. Requests for chalk and erasers—the same. Yet the book closet held none of these materials. Requests for help with students were answered by suggestions to call the student's parents, or chat with the guidance counselor. Parents answered Rodney's calls with anger, and the guidance counselor scoffed at the problem. Rodney felt betrayed. What had happened?

Rodney's administrator expected him to work within the traditional structures of the school. This administrator judged Rodney's success or failure on the same basis that he used to judge the other teachers: Rodney was expected to perform within the norms of the department; Rodney was to act like an innovative problem-solver, not a beginner dependent on a department chair; Rodney was expected, like the other teachers, to handle the crises one day at a time, not to come running for help. To the extent that Rodney could successfully and happily operate within his own classroom, his administrator judged that he was doing a professional job; to the extent that Rodney begged for help, his administrator judged that Rodney was not up to snuff.

How Do You Recognize a Trustworthy Administrator?

Generally she will make you feel good about your work and secure in your position. She will help you organize a project and reward your efforts with appreciation. Any skillful technician can organize the paper supplies and book orders with alacrity, but a skillful personnel manager will assist the teachers to achieve success in all aspects of their work. A good administrator keeps you informed about your job prospects in an honest and forthright manner. If your department enjoys amicable working relations among its members, you are probably working for a good administrator because she does not cause the department members to compete internally against each other.

If you find that your administrator respects you and encourages you to do what you do best, then you have found one of the gems of the education profession. Nonetheless, play your professional role professionally: Be discreet, and thank your lucky stars that you have been blessed with a supportive administrator on your way to becoming a successful teacher.

THE ADMINISTRATIVE RHYTHM

The surprise is that the step of administrative rhythm does not coincide with the pace of the teacher's teaching year. Reflect on this and, after you have gained some experience, you will be able to work out a strategy that allows you to adapt to the two schedules: the teaching/learning schedule on the one hand, and the administrative schedule on the other.

One difference between the two schedules is evaluation. Whereas most teachers and students evaluate their success or failure during the school year towards the end of the year, administrators, planning for the next school year, begin evaluating in the fall. Why is this? Administrative work involves the coordination of several academic departments, and it takes a great deal of time. Administrators oversee the publication of course catalogues, they coordinate guidance work, they design budgets, they act as trouble-shooters for the day-to-day functioning of their schools, and they do a lot more, little of it having to do with the actual teaching and learning process in which the teachers and students are dutifully engaging.

Administrators concentrate on evaluating actual classroom teaching less than you might imagine. Not surprisingly, the impressions you make during the first few months of the school year will probably have more influence over ultimate administrative decisions about you than you realize. Your informal evaluation, therefore, begins from the first day of school. The reputation you establish in the fall will carry you, or plague you, throughout the year. Build your reputation by doing what you do best and then by communicating effectively with your administrative staff about your successes.

Another of the shocking discords between the teaching and learning rhythms and the administrative rhythm—and there are many—is that moment when students are required to meet with their guidance counselors during the first half of the year to plan their following year's schedule. How can they possibly decide what to take next year when they have hardly had time to see how they handle this year's courses? Often, teachers are asked to give recommendations for students who are new to their classes. This is the administrative calendar at work on its own terms.

HOW TO BLOW YOUR OWN HORN QUIETLY

Because these administrative types who are now in charge of your future career in this school district operate on their own time schedule, which differs from yours, you need to be aware of the rhythm of the administrative calendar for the sake of your own self-protection. If you know when decisions are to be made about evaluating your work, you can participate in shaping your own future.

Likewise, you need to know that they depend on information about your work gathered not only from their own observations made directly in your classes and from school gossip—that all-important source of infallible knowledge—but also from what you yourself say to them about yourself. Administrators are always eager to hear about the successes that you are enjoying. To know that you are doing well makes them feel justified in having hired you.

Build your own reputation by actively doing the kind of teaching that you are good at, that you know will be highly appreciated, and then let your administrators know about it. If you share your successes on a regular basis with your school administrators, you are bound to shape the kind of reputation that you want to have.

Do not be timid about talking to the principal about your new project. He will be pleased to hear your good news. Most likely, you were hired based on your academic strength or promise or experience that made you seem valuable and viable. When you design projects, write up proposals, and structure classes that build upon those strengths, fulfill that promise, and recycle your experience—and then, when you do an effective job of letting the right people know—you are doing what has to be done to build a teaching career.

One new teacher, who had majored in Latin American Cultures, designed an art project that brought together social studies teachers, language teachers, and art teachers to help students learn about architecture and culture in Latin America. Another neophyte invited her math professor from the local university to speak before the Math Club. Fostering the collaboration of your peers, and connecting your school with the larger world surrounding it, are two styles of career-building that you can count on to work.

Caveat! Collegiality and equality among teachers is one of the more pleasant social facts of educational life; therefore, gushing about every effective lesson you teach can be boring and unnerving to seasoned teachers. Experienced teachers know the pitfalls of every kind of project. They have probably even tried every kind of project, including the one that you think you just invented. You are a rookie whose teaching peers form opinions about you in all kinds of ways that differ from the administrative evaluation. You don't need to hide what you are doing, but don't brag about it either. In fact, you will probably learn more about the culture and reality of your school—not to mention teaching itself—if you spend more time listening to your colleagues and less time telling them about everything you are doing in your classes.

SCHOOL POLITICS: Presenting Yourself as a Professional

Your students are not the only ones who undergo exams and get grades. Some time during the first couple of months, you will probably receive your first visit from the observers and the evaluators. Surprisingly—or not so surprisingly—the administrators who make these official observations of you laboring at your craft almost always know their opinions of you before they walk into your room. The grapevine of your school will take care of that.

Look for clues in what they say to you. Some districts purposely require observers to put in negative comments to give them "fair grounds" for not rehiring you in the event—for whatever other reasons—they decide that they want to let you go. Other districts require administrators to be critical in order to prove that they are doing their jobs.

No matter what they say, grin and bear it. Show sincere interest in improving your performance, even if you disagree with the evaluator. If you are not sure whether your evaluation is negative or positive, invite your evaluator back to your classroom. The second evaluation will tell you whether you are being given the beginner's treatment, or your low marks reflect some aspect of your teaching that you do truly need to improve.

As a new teacher, you will be observed by administrators on an administrative rhythmic basis, that is, at their convenience, not yours. Each school district has its own set of procedures concerning formal or informal evaluations. The latter may involve the evaluator's "dropping by" for a few minutes or an entire class, but does not necessarily involve a formal write-up or evaluation form. Find out when these casual observations are liable to occur by asking veteran teachers. Or keep your ears open when other teachers begin to comment that they have just been observed: You'll be next. In most schools, the formal written observations are made late in the fall and again in mid-spring. The new teacher can be prepared for the evaluator's stated arrival in the knowledge that evaluators often wait until the last minute.

Many evaluations are quite painless, and they can even be rewarding for your work and your progress towards success as a teacher. But beware of the evaluations that make you feel unappreciated and misunderstood. Moreover, a sudden negative change in tone from one evaluation to the next can mean that your evaluator does not plan to rehire you. When that happens, then is the time to start looking for another job. The final evaluation formally communicates to you whether or not you will be rehired.

Do not panic over a less-than-enthusiastic write-up. Rather than fighting a negative evaluation, make every effort to find out why the evaluator was critical. Most systems allow you only to write a rebuttal to a critical evaluation rather than permitting the removal of a mistake or misunderstanding. If you become sure that the relationship between you and your evaluators is souring, ask them for suggestions, modify your classrom practice, and think seriously about looking for another job.

E IS FOR EVALUATION

You can help shape the evaluations of your work to produce the positive decision that you are hoping for when rehiring time comes in the spring. Share your successes by informing your chair and your principal, by writing notices for intraschool bulletins, and by posting displays of work outside your classroom. From the first day of school, actively seek out opportunities to perform in arenas where your talents and qualities will shine to your best advantage. Select one after-school activity in which you are interested with which to assist. Take part in the social life of your new school—this gives you the advantage of getting to know your students and your fellow teachers outside the limits of the academic environment in the classroom. By February, your reputation will have been set, and so probably will your future (or lack of one) at this school.

Some administrators are required to include negative comments or "areas to be improved" in your evaluation as reminders to themselves (and to you) that the "perfect" teacher does not exist (and that no untenured teacher's job is "safe.") Even though you may never achieve an altogether glowing evaluation (even though you might well deserve it), and despite how you may feel about this unfair treatment, remain outwardly cheerful at work, and discuss only the good points about your job and your positive feelings. Until you get tenure, and even afterwards, operate in a business-like manner. Evaluate your prospects rationally and act accordingly. Use job-hunting opportunities as a way to inform yourself about other districts, while keeping your local options open in your own school district.

Andrew made a mistake: Andrew didn't keep his ear to the ground. In Andrew's school, each teacher had an office with a telephone. Preparation periods were spent alone or in consultation with students. The faculty room was hardly used at all. Andrew discovered that small cliques of teachers met in their offices, but because he was new, Andrew was not yet a member of any of the in-groups. Andrew never heard any school gossip; he felt lonely. He heard whispers about changes in the school, but he found it a long and difficult process to uncover the poltical realities and rhythms of this school. And in the end, without allies and because he had neither found a way to see and be seen, nor hear and be heard, Andrew's evaluation contained a lot of "areas to be improved."

You will soon learn about your own limitations, but do not discuss these with administrators. You need their good opinion in order to succeed at your school. Otherwise, you may find your own confession about a classroom failure reappearing in your written evaluation where it can be used against you. It is manipulative—we admit—not only to find ways to publicize your achievements but also to suppress your feelings and comments about your failures, your struggles, and your inadequacies. Do it anyway! Don't lie; we are not suggesting that you say anything untrue; we are merely saying that you serve your own purposes best by emphasizing your strengths and keeping your weaknesses to yourself. Ought you to register truthful, objective, sober complaints about lack of support? Insufficient materials? Lack of space? Too little time? No! *No! NO!*

Why not? The savvy answer is a political one: You do not want to embarrass your superiors, especially over a matter in which they may be helpless, anyway. You are working within space, with materials, and according to time constraints that your administrators structured during the previous year. When you, the new teacher, came on the scene in the fall, you walked into a pre-set situation which your administrators, now, have little power to change. If you complain—especially if your complaints are accurate—you may make them feel frustrated with you because you are making obvious what they failed to foresee or otherwise did not accomplish. Don't carp; cope!

If you are short on textbooks, have to teach in four different classrooms, have never seen a file cabinet, and some of your classes are tiny but most of them are way too large—all these factors, for good or ill, were set the year before you came. By all means, inquire politely if there is money in the budget for the needed books or other materials, but when they tell you "No," do not register your surprise. Instead, watch and listen carefully to find out how and when your colleagues wangle the materials they want, and go thou and do likewise. Schools, even private schools, often allocate supplies more generously to those who know how and when to ask.

Rose, a first-year Spanish teacher, was overwhelmed by her nightly duties of planning different lessons and correcting classwork and homework assignments for over one-hundred students. She grew increasingly on edge with her family at home and with her students at school. In a meeting with her supervisor, Rose mentioned her feeling of being overwhelmed by her daily workload. Later, an experienced language teacher saw Rose's distress, and she advised her to spot-check homework and class assignments, explaining that no language teacher in the department could handle as much correcting as Rose was struggling to do. Soon, Rose had mastered her new grading system, and she was feeling much better about everything. Rose shared her new successes with her supervisor. In Rose's end-of-the-year evaluation, she noticed that her supervisor had written that "Rose at times seemed to be overwhelmed by her assignment." Never mind that Rose had triumphed! Never mind that growing pains led on to strength and maturity! If Rose had not admitted to her earlier struggles, the supervisor could not have carried the negative impression into the evaluation.

Sometimes colleagues will tell you that the school will retain you if you have done a good job. If you believe in that idealistic promise in these days of budget crises and declining enrollments, then you are setting yourself up for a broken heart. Even though you may do the best you can possibly do, and even though you may outshine every other new teacher who ever walked through the door of your school, you may nevertheless join the ranks of those many fine teachers who have lost positions because there were just not enough classes to go round in the coming year.

Learn the law of the labor market: When there is a teacher shortage, it is easy to retain your job; it's a seller's market, and you've got the goods. When there is a glut of teachers, it is easy for administrators to let you go, even if just to see who else is available. Last hired, first fired. If you are in this position, and if the axe falls, it is not a negative reflection on you either personally or professionally, but that doesn't keep it from hurting. Your main protection is to understand what is going on.

Teachers at all schools shape their environment by setting up pecking orders and storing up the collective historical memory of past slights and traumas. Any school that has experienced a strike or student upheaval will have its share of teachers who talk about these events for years afterward. In personal matters as well, oral traditions are powerful within school communities. Many teachers celebrate whole lifetimes of love affairs, divorces, marriages, births, and deaths together. Faculty relations are unique in each school, and predictably common everywhere, but they are inevitably important shapers of the reality and the possibilities of teaching.

A final word on evaluations, self- and other-: Yes, the evaluation by your administrators determines your future in this school—whether or not you get rehired for next year. But no, what this or that administrator thinks of you personally and professionally does not determine your entire career as a teacher, and you must not let others' opinions determine what you think of yourself. Pick the roses and leave the thorns: If someone says something useful to you, keep it; if someone says something useless or hurtful, throw it away.

Throughout your career, you yourself are going to be the toughest evaluator of your own work. You will know best what your talents are and in which new ways you might grow. Be your own evaluator, and be cautious either of using formal evaluations as ego boosters or suffering them as professional disasters. Teachers must build an inner confidence in themselves. Every teacher knows that there is not one "best" teaching style or an "ideal" teacher, yet it is probable that every teacher would actually like to be given just that compliment. One of the toughest parts about becoming a teacher—like one of the toughest parts about life—is that the process never ends. On the other hand, that's also one of the best parts.

Mentors

Many schools are now providing trained peer coaches or mentors for teachers new to the system or district. Mentors can sometimes be as hard to get along with as are some uncooperative teacher colleagues and obstinate administrators. You may end up depending on your mentor for what were traditionally the tasks of the administrator, and if so, then your mentor may be a useful supply line of information.

The function of the mentor is to meet regularly to answer questions, solve problems, and provide help untying the knots described in this book. Mentors are often either paid extra for their services or given released time from teaching. Mentors may also observe the new teachers at work in classes, and generally they help them adjust to the system as quickly as possible. Prior to the advent of official mentoring, teachers often found their own informal ways of mentoring each other. Teachers who came into the system at the same time, for example, would discuss their mutual concerns.

M IS FOR MENTOR

When mentoring works well, it provides you with a person you can trust, and an environment in which you can unburden yourself of your problems and concerns, and celebrate your triumphs, without fear of negative professional repercussions. Mentoring is usually effective because mentors have volunteered for the task, and a natural weeding process has rooted out the burned-out, bitter teachers.

The best mentor is a friend, ready, willing, and able to show you the ropes. The worst mentors are jealous and destructive. Normally, however, mentors just don't care very much or make much time for you.

We advise: Handle all relationships during your first year— mentors included—with poise, with wit, and with a grain of salt.

Peer-coaching and mentoring are similar in function, although —as the word "peer" implies—peer coaches are equal in status to each other. In peer-coaching, two teachers choose to work together; they observe each other in their classrooms and strive to help one another understand their respective successes and failures. Whereas mentoring takes place between an older, abler, more experienced teacher and a younger one, peer coaching is more egalitarian, and it is therefore less threatening. You may not want to get involved in a peer-coaching experience until after you have gained tenure, or at the very least until you know who your friends are. Your school, however, may require you to become involved in peer-coaching before tenure has been granted; if this is so, try to make sure that your peer coach is trustworthy, before you show all your cards.

And finally, there's the help you can do without, the attentions of the wolf in wolf's clothing. One form of unofficial mentoring in your first year will probably be the teacher or administrator of the opposite sex who is interested in you whereas you do not feel any reciprocal feelings: Sexual harrasment? Maybe; maybe not.

You may be new and you may be young, but you don't have to be a victim. Deal with unwelcome attention as reprehensible sexual harassment, and take the same steps that you would take in any other situation. Don't be embarrassed to say "No!" If the harassment continues, then do not be afraid to explain your problem to an administrator or a representative of the union.

We observe that out-and-out sexual harassment is actually rare in schools. When it does occur, it is usually based on unequal power relations; power plays, however, are not usually an issue among teachers, although administrators may be a different matter. In teaching, women share the same postions as men, and seldom are you typed by gender. One of the fringe benefits of teaching is that sexual harassment is not so frequent in schools as it is in the business world.

THE UNION: To Join, or Not to Join

Unions prove confusing to many new teachers. Unions have numerous negative associations in folklore, mythology, and labor history. They are seen as self-serving institutions that promote feather-bedding, that protect tenured but dead-wood teachers who are not doing a good job, and that put teachers in the category not of intellectual or professional but of industrial laborer.

Unions, nonetheless, are now a powerful force in the world of education. Unions set labor conditions in terms of pay and working environment; even in schools where there is no union, the good influence of teachers organized for their own professional sakes can be felt. Although non-tenured teachers have very little protection under union contracts and state laws, many unions serve as pressure groups and interest lobbies within school districts in ways that benefit all teachers. Like them or not, unions are often actual players in the political life of the school. So if you want to know who has power in your school, follow those issues in which the union takes part.

"Should I join the teachers'union?"

Many schools are "closed shop," and you become a union member automatically; your dues are deducted from your salary. In any case, if there is a union, you want to join it. No other organization speaks and acts as forcefully on your behalf as a good union does. Because you're new on the job, hold your tongue in any conversations about the union. You may find that you change your mind in either direction about the role of your teachers' union.

Read your union contract to find out about your salary schedule. Does your pay depend on your taking courses? Plan your coursework so that you will arrive at the maximum pay step as fast as you can.

Find out who is active in your union. What does the union do that you are interested in? During your first year, keep quiet and observe! Later on, after you have tenure, you may find that you have become a union activist! Teachers need all the help they can get, and especially they need to stick together.

U IS FOR UNION

The bureaucratic systems in your school are often the most difficult puzzles for new teachers to figure out. Schools of Education seldom, if ever, offer either theoretical acknowledgment of their existence or practical guidance in how to negotiate them. Nonetheless, no teachers—neither the new and inexperienced nor the old hands—can afford to be ignorant of this fact of school life.

The insights we offer are based on our experiences. Compare these vignettes with your own circumstances, and then make your own decisions about how to proceed. Awareness of political realities and professional connections in your school gives you the power to control your own environment and enables you to experience freedom among choices, determining where and when you want to fit in smoothly or choose to buck the tide.

KIDS

You're there because of the kids. School is *about* a lot of things, but it's *for* them. If kids are a bother to you, if you can't tolerate their childish ways, if you feel put upon for having to put up with their nonsense, then you ought not to be a teacher. If, on the other hand, you are passionate about kids and their learning, then you'll make a great teacher.

In this chapter, we assume your successes with well-planned lessons and responsible students. We know that you will enjoy your share of rewards with your classes, but what about the thorny situations with seemingly insuperable difficulties? With these problems, teachers need all the help they can get.

At a school where Mindy started her career teaching ninth- and tenth-graders, she had to cope with silliness, group taunting of individuals, and the inability of most of her students to comprehend any abstract ideas. She warned her colleague who taught the 11th- and 12th-graders about the crazy behavior he could expect in the next year's crop, but the next year, Mindy's colleague said that his new students were calm and well-behaved. After a couple more years, Mindy eventually realized that her 9th-grade babies and 10th-grade lamebrains had actually matured on their way to becoming upperclassmen. Mindy learned to relax, she began to laugh at her kids' childishness, and it dawned on her that there might even have been some point in reading all that stuff by Piaget on "stages" that she had been assigned back during her Ed. course work. Mindy included new lessons in which her students were allowed to use their bodies to act-out and play-act the material she taught. She employed the learning styles appropriate to the maturity level of 9th- and 10th-graders to teach the content she had been unsuccessfully trying to get across by fussing at them about being "more mature." Mindy even came round to liking their excitability and wide-open questions about the world around them. As the years went by, she came to relish her students' precisely honed questions, such as "Is reincarnation possible?" and "But why don't we do away with poverty?" and "How can I make my personality better?" And the person who gained maturity in this process was Mindy herself.

Note the learning styles of all your students, but especially those who require special assistance. Improved testing techniques can identify students who need extra time, visual presentations in addition to oral teaching, and the full range of other learning modes. You can help your students achieve by learning as much as you can about how they learn.

Many students with learning disabilities have special difficulties: Some have organizational problems—they lose their books all the time (as well as their place in your lesson); some have problems processing information—they hear you, but they can't make sense of what you are saying. Usually, students with learning disabilities can benefit from sitting in the front of the class where you can easily point to materials on their desks while you are verbally telling the rest of the class. Some students who are easily distracted are often put at ease by sitting close to someone in authority who is calm.

Ready awareness of special medical needs is crucial. Devise a code for your grade book or attendance list to keep you reminded that someone has a special need. Jo-ann, the young English teacher whom we mentioned before, in "Systems," received an administrative memo on the first day of school in September that one of her students was diabetic, and she was instructed to destroy this confidential notice. When Jo-ann got to know the student, she was amused by his punk-rock style and the tough-guy demeanor that camouflaged his lively intelligence and keen curiosity. Had Jo-ann done more than merely do what she was told and destroy the note, had she noted her punker's special health need, she might have known what to do during the final exam in May when he had his diabetic attack.

Kids actually are young humans, and teaching them is alluring if for no other reason than because you never really get all aspects of your role as teacher exactly right. In the process of teaching, you sometimes achieve a transcendent moment (while relishing together a character in fiction or seeing together the solution to a complex equation) during which you sense that you are doing the job you were trained to do, fulfilling the call by which you were called to become a teacher. In the give and take with your students, you are taking part in that universal process by which adults pass down the wisdom of the ages to the next generation.

K IS FOR KIDS

KIDS AND KEEPING YOUR SENSE OF HUMOR

The ways you feel about your students and your daily interactions with them are ever changing. Teaching is a tough job, and each day will leave you with many experiences to mull over. Teachers' spouses and friends have often been known to beg for surcease from all the teaching stories they get to hear week after week: "No, I don't care what Joey said to you about his reasons for failing your last test!"

Your main instructive task is to set up an environment in your classroom in which your students will delight in learning. If you do it right, they will feel free to explore, challenged to think things through, disciplined to learn with precision. You will be making it possible for them both to master bodies of knowledge and the skills of learning and knowing. One of the best modes in which to accomplish all of this is to keep a good sense of humor.

Your main emotional task is to give yourself and your students space to be yourselves and still be able to appreciate one another. Mutual good humor with each other is imperative because you live together day after day. You are the grown-up, and they are growing up. When you teach a student as a freshman and then again as a senior, you will observe tremendous changes that have taken place in appearance and personality. You will be able to congratulate yourself for having been one of the helpful hands that pointed and pulled, pushed and patted and applauded as another fellow human lurched forward towards maturity. Deal with your teenagers' grandiose notions and conceited actions with a dash of humor. Balance your younger children's wild imaginations and over-earnestness

L IS FOR LAUGHTER

with your own kind whimsy. Younger and older students alike will expect you to be rock-steady because they need your reliability in the face of their own shaky experiences growing up. Accept them and their foibles with good humor, and they might once in a while extend the same good will towards you!

COPING WITH PROBLEM KIDS

Some kids have bigger problems than you can handle. Sometimes, situations in classrooms build and build until they get out of hand, and you—outnumbered and single-handed—cannot be expected to be a combination of the U.S. Cavalry, Mary Poppins, and a Saturday-morning television Superhero. Two good ways to cope are (a) keep your own feelings out of it, and (b) know how and when to call for help.

Keeping your personal emotional reactions separate from appropriately professional, teacherly reactions is a matter of practicality and technique. One technique is called "documenting"—you go to the trouble to keep daily records of class incidents or unusual behaviors.

One teacher we know keeps a small piece of paper clipped inside her attendance book, a new and dated sheet for each day; she saves these sheets in a folder. If an incident occurs in her class that she might want to remember to recount in a conference with a student or a counselor or a parent, she jots it down immediately but briefly during classtime. To keep her note-taking as quick as possible, she's even developed a short-hand code for typical, repeated behaviors such as "interrupting others" or "failing to bring materials to class."

The process of writing the behaviors down on a daily basis helps our teacher-friend put aside her own emotional reactions; her written record of the incident allows her to put her own feelings about it on a back burner while she continues the business of the class. Students notice when she pauses to write, and occasionally her pause to write is enough to help poorly behaved students reconsider their actions. She does not stop to discuss why she is jotting down these notes, however. She says: "We are not going to discuss this just now," but she has made clear outside of class what she was doing and why.

Although this documenting technique sounds similar to the old teacher ploy of threatening to give zeroes for poor behavior, it can also be used in a positive and supportive way to help reflect to the student in a private meeting exactly how that student was behaving in class. Many students, like many grown-ups, do not realize how often, and in what ways, they behave inappropriately. If you are considering discussing a student's problems with other adults, such as guidance counselors or disciplinary authorities or parents, this daily record documents an objective presentation of the problem.

Even though documenting can be mistaken and misused, it is far better than relying on faulty memory and emitting an emotional howl: "This kid is just ruining my class!" Daily notations reinforce your abililty to be accurate, settle your nerves, and give you a sense of being able to cope with onging problems.

IN THE MIDDLE BETWEEN THE KIDS AND THE ADMINISTRATORS

As a teacher, you are a model of adult behavior before your students. You teach them to work by demonstrating industry in your own actions. You teach them a love of learning by being yourself a lifelong learner. You teach them social and interpersonal skills by the way that you react and respond to them. Therefore, your first requirement in class is to be able to have space and time to be the example you want to be. If the emotional needs of your students interfere with your ability to function, you must find ways to eliminate, or at least to minimize, this drain on your energies. When you find that students cannot control their behavior despite your assistance and insistence, or when their own personal problems overwhelm them so that they cannot function either in or out of your class, you need to call for outside help.

All schools provide support services for students, such as guidance counselors, deans, social workers, or administrators in charge of student behavior or discipline. Sometimes the bureaucratic names for these roles become Orwellian in the tendency to name the role as the opposite of its function: e.g. calling a disciplinarian a "vice-principal," or a guidance counselor a "dean." You need to observe the general tone and style of your own school so that you may know whether official job titles are descriptive of the actual roles that the office-holders perform, and under which circumstances you actually may, and ought to, refer students to the support staff.

Administrators usually have a very limited range of powers within which to ameliorate tough situations in students' lives. If you can suggest a logical and clear solution, it will make the administrative task easier. Because teachers usually deal with administrators in stressful, sometimes distressing, situtations, however, be hesitant to get involved in this way during your first year in a new school. You must keep your ears and eyes open, you must observe the customary practices and regulations in your school, and you must live to fight again another day. It takes learned experience to be able to handle your kids and your administrators adroitly.

This is a tricky process. Some schools develop a punitive atmosphere in which students are "sent to the office" to be yelled at and punished, but most schools have developed sophisticated social-service mechanisms that distinguish discipline matters from problem students with emotional distress. If your school includes a social worker or a drug counselor, find out how to refer students to them. Ask if you can make referrals anonymously.

Although magic solutions are rare for the severe problems that some students may have, if they are directed to professional help, and if you have the opportunity to lend a hand, you should do so. You cannot help everyone, but you can take advantage of whatever assistance there is available in your school. You may end up rescuing someone without ever knowing all the details about what happened.

THE POLITICS OF DISCIPLINE

Administrators in a school are ultimately responsible to parents and the School Superintendent and the School Board for decisions regarding your students. Most often, school administrators deal with only the most important disciplinary decisions, or they act as a last-resort court of appeal to adjudicate matters that vitally concern a student's school career. Administrators have the power to punish by suspension or expulsion from school; therefore, the pressures on them are different from the ones on you. On the one hand, administrators are responsible to set the boundaries of acceptable behavior within your school; on the other, they have the political desire to build unblemished reputations in order to protect their own careers. Administrators most often wish that you, the teacher, would handle every problem on your own so that they would not have to be accountable at all; therefore, be careful when you take a problem to a school administrator.

The first step towards getting help for a student in trouble is to familiarize yourself with the official procedures of your new school. What do the administrators actually tell you is available for you? In the effort to find out what is really available, go ahead and ask everyone what school procedure is. If your colleagues express opinions about school procedures different from what is stated in official guidelines, then your school has unwritten, customary codes which you need to learn.

Caveat! A new teacher who uses support services more than other teachers do, is communicating to the administration that she or he has classroom control problems. Even if you do actually have these problems, broadcasting them to the entire bureaucracy of the school is not in your own, or your students', best interests.

RECONNOITERING THE TERRAIN: Your Allies

Guidance Counselors

Guidance counselors and teachers have a lot in common: They are both overworked and underpaid, loaded down with more kids than they can help. Secondary-school counselors are often responsible for two hundred or more students across four or more classes from freshmen to seniors. A lone middle-school counselor may be responsible for every kid in the fifth through the eighth grade. Counselors schedule each student for the next year's classes; they interact privately with each of their advisees at least once or twice per year; they hold conferences with parents, adminstrators, and teachers. They meet with adminstrative personnel over student issues and school policy. They send periodic mailings to students and parents to inform them of school policy and procedures. They are responsible for all student records, and they do college and career counseling. They also do personal and family counseling.

G IS FOR GUIDANCE COUNSELOR

Like teachers, guidance counselors are professionally trained and licensed. Within school systems, however, guidance counselors appear to occupy a higher status than do teachers because they have their own offices and telephones, and they share secretarial services that are not available to teachers. Most importantly, counselors are not subject to the demanding daily time and performance schedules that define the teacher's existence. In many schools, guidance counselors have "risen through the ranks" out of the teaching profession. They are teachers with a Master's degree in guidance; therefore, they appear to have been promoted.

Guidance departments, however, rarely have control over either school policies or teachers. Because the counselors are not classroom educators, they function only as support staff ancillary to the rest of the system. For this reason, guidance counselors rarely have any input on evaluations of your performance as a teacher. Your relationship with them is usually not subject to the kinds of professional pressures that you might experience with other administrators who also evaluate you.

Unlike teachers, guidance counselors use their phones frequently to check with parents, administrators, and teachers. During certain periods of the school year, typically in the fall and spring, they are deluged with problems and requests that require quick resolutions. Like teachers, they experience the driving rhythms of a school year that call upon them for resilience.

Guidance counselors, in most events, are likely to be your best bet when you need to reach out to find help for a student. New teachers, however, sometimes expect too much from the guidance counselors. No matter how competent the counselors may be, they cannot resolve your students' problems as fast as you might like. Moreover, the student-guidance counselor is not YOUR counselor. If you are in distress or upset over a situation with one of your students, do not expect the counselors either to reassure you or help you work it out. Your problems are not their job.

Assume nothing at the start of the year about anyone's willingness or ability to be helpful to students with special problems. Meet each counselor individually before you decide whether or not to request help with a student. Occasionally you will find school personnel who will gladly leave you holding the bag. Do not expect either the couselors or the administration necessarily to jump to your defense in an altercation with parents or with a troubled student. Before you wade into a murky situation, make sure that you can count on the back-up you will need from your colleagues and administrators. Look before you leap!

José, a second-year teacher, was having problems in a senior economics class. One student came late to class, brought neither notebook nor pencil, made rude comments, walked out of class at his leisure, and insulted José to his face. José noted down these behaviors for a week, and then—following school procedures—José filled out a "discipline referral form." He felt relieved that at last he would have some back-up enforcement of his class rules.

When José got no response from the administration, José asked why. The administrator in question asked José whether the student ever swore at him in class. When José hesitantly answered, "No, but he has been exceedingly rude," the administrator replied: "If he swears at you, be sure to let me know." José had learned that in this school, administrators discipline students who swear, not students who are merely rude.

You must take care to protect both yourself and your student when you enlist the aid of your school, whether guidance counselors or the principal or vice-principals, to deal with special problems. In some situations, you may find that your school guidance people are no help at all, either in providing information to you or advising your students.

Occasionally a counselor is mismatched by personality with a student. They just don't like or understand each other. Once in a while, overworked and overwrought counselors blame the students for bringing their problems upon themselves, and sometimes a counselor will blame a teacher for bringing in a student with a problem. When a counselor puts both you and the student on the defensive, it is not likely to be a productive meeting.

Tread carefully. Go into every situation with a counselor with the trust that the counselor will be truly professional with both you and the student. In any given situation, you may see things differently from the way the counselor does. Rely on the counselor as far as you can, and cooperate with the counselor as much as you can. Take whatever independent action that you must, but never try to change the counselor's mind! Then you will have two problems: a troubled student and a resentful counselor.

The counselor may put the student's problem on the bottom of her list, whereas it is at the top of yours. For example, you may have a student in a class who is grossly misplaced: He is failing tests because he is not prepared for your course, and you know that he should be switched into a more appropriate class immediately. The counselor, however, preoccupied with very many other tasks—some of them quite possibly more important than the problem your student is having—may not have time to deal with your situation right away. Thus, you will be forced to learn patience and forebearance or to find another solution to your problem. Assure the student that the problem will be resolved as soon as possible; suggest that he politely pursue the matter with the counselor. One of the jobs they did not prepare you for in the School of Education is teaching your students how to get the help they need from their own counselors.

Student Files

The guidance office controls students' files; it's up to you to find out school policy and practice in the use of these private sources of information about your students. Some teachers believe that reading student records prejudices their treatment of students because the teachers are tempted to accept as predictive what previous teachers have said about the students. Former teachers' evaluations can prejudice you in favor of, or against, a student. Teachers who forego reading student records believe that they should deal with each student anew, providing them with a clean slate.

We disagree: It's your slate—not the student's—that is wiped clean, and you are left with little information about why and how a student acts out. When used properly, the information you can derive by reading students' records truly enhances your ability to respond to students' individual, peculiar needs. In schools where you are officially not allowed to read student transcripts, you can gain the helpful information that you need by asking guidance counselors for personal background profiles on students, their test scores, former evaluations, information about their family situations, and the patterns of their entire school careers. Many students have personality problems that were evident as early as kindergarten. You may discover, for example, that a withdrawn student is a loner who has been reported to behave this way since entering school. With that information, you can better understand that student's behavior in your classroom—and not take it personally when the student misbehaves.

A new teacher named Geoff thought that one of his students was challenging him in class because Geoff was a novice teacher. When Geoff perused his student's guidance file, however, he found that many mid-term progress reports had been filed with complaints from other teachers about similar behavior: The student had an *attitude* that made him confrontational. Geoff's problem was in his student, not with himself. Geoff was relieved, and now he was able to discuss with a counselor and some other teachers the techniques with which Geoff might hope to help his student change his behavior.

Sometimes, you even discover positive comments in the records that put you in touch with your students' histories. Then you can encourage them to keep going towards achievement in your class along tracks that they have found smooth before. Sometimes, you can catch a learning disability that has gone unrecognized. Sometimes, you can learn about problems—at home or elsewhere outside of school—over which a student has no control, but in regards to which your awareness will make you a better teacher and friend.

Because the guidance counselor's special status as private advisor to any student is a privileged one, you can rely on the guidance personnel for special assistance when you sense the need to help a student outside of your classroom. You may ask the guidance counselor, for example, to arrange a three-, four-, or five-way conference among yourself, the counselor, the student, and—perhaps—a parent (or parents) and/or other teachers. This is what Mary, a new teacher, did after she finally figured out how the process worked in her school.

Unbeknownst to Mary, the student she was concerned about had a history of minor drug violations. An assiduous reader of the weekly attendance bulletin, Mary discovered that this student, who had been missing class a lot, was on a dismissal list for seven consecutive Fridays. Mary conscientiously went to the guidance counselor's office to ask what had caused all the dismissals.

The guidance counselor's secretary pulled open her top drawer and tossed about seventy excuse notes on her desk. The counselor then emerged from her office and suggested that Mary sort through the notes, find the relevant ones, and call the student's parents. The counselor implied that this was standard procedure. Mary sorted through the notes, including some that had been signed by the boy's mother, and then one evening she called their home.

On the phone, the boy's mother became outraged. She demanded to know why Mary hadn't informed her of these dismissals earlier. She claimed that she'd never written the notes. She called the principal the following day to complain about Mary's failure to inform her of the repeated absences. Embarrassed that her son had been pulling the wool over her eyes, the mother displaced her anger at her son and vented her frustration on the teacher.

Mary felt humiliated, even though it was through her own efforts that the student's duplicity was discovered. The boy had been leaving school early to take drugs. The next day, Mary took the problem back to the guidance counselor, who had access to the boy's full record and knew more about his misdeeds than Mary had known. Mary needed to discover how to make an ally of the busy guidance counselor. She might have requested a four-way meeting with the counselor, the student, and the parent, to allow the truth to come out.

The lessons to be learned from Mary's situation are many: Guidance counselors and their secretaries don't always do it right. There are more kids and more teachers and more problems than they have time or energy to deal with in the best possible way. Sometimes, it's up to you to help them, if you want to help that kid.

On the other hand, let the guidance counselor make as many of the phone calls to parents as possible. You can assume nothing about the relationships that students have with their parents.

One of the most agonizing problems that teachers face is when their students must cope with problems that seem almost unsolvable— for instance, a student with low learning ability, whose parents are putting pressure on their child to succeed in a demanding class. Students suffering from physical illness, mental depression, death or other tragedy at home, and the ill effects of pandemic divorce/remarriage/complex families, and the whole range of other problems of modern American life, often have great difficulty concentrating in school. Even though we try to keep the school environment as civil as we can, sometimes students have great difficulty operating in any social setting. You will need to learn to forgive your students, the school guidance personnel, and yourself for being unable to find a solution that works for every student every year.

Other Allies

Your other allies are the Learning Specialists, Social Workers, ESL Teachers, the School Nurse, and the Drug Counselor. Have we left anybody out? You yourself may be one of these specialists who assists students in adjusting to their school environments, and we don't want to leave you out. School support personnel are crucially important in any school, though not every school is fortunate enough to have a full staff of specialized helpers.

Specialists have information about students that all classroom teachers need to know. Many school districts now require detailed reporting to classroom teachers about all students who receive special help outside of the academic classes. If your school does not make this requirement, take it upon yourself to contact any teachers who work with your students: Communicate regularly about their progress and their special needs. Whether you are a classroom teacher or a specialist, you are a member of a professional team whose only job is to help your students. Learn to work together.

KIDS OUTSIDE THE CLASSROOM

If you teach in the upper grades, you will be instructing anywhere from twenty to thirty-five students up to five times each day. If you teach in the lower grades, you will probably have approximately thirty kids—the same kids all day long every day. Besides your role of being "the teacher," you will have other responsibilities, as well: hall duty, lunch duty, study-hall duty among them. You may be advising a club or coaching a team. You will be planning, grading, and designing tests. You will be organizing and conducting group activities. On top of teaching from different sections of different texts each day, you will be finding time to assess each student's academic progress and emotional state.

How are you going to find time and energy to accomplish all this? How do you know when you need outside help in dealing with your students?

If you want to make a commitment to teaching your students as full human beings, rather than as mere students, you must be careful to understand the emotional and time constraints and the political realities under which you will be operating. Once you are aware of the realities, you will be better able to calculate under which conditions and circumstances you wish—and can afford—to go beyond your classroom relationships with your students. Most of the out-of-class time you spend with students will probably be fun. You can laugh with them and get to know them by talking about your common interests. Sometimes, however, students will approach you to talk seriously about complex, troublesome, and even dangerous problems that they are facing.

As you gain experience, you will develop a sense of when and where intervention in students' problems can be of benefit. You will also develop the ability to discern which complexities to try to help unravel, which troubles to try to heal, which dangers to try to help avoid, and whether or not you will intervene at all.

If you are considering becoming involved in a student's out-of-school life, you need to decide whether you can afford to take the time to act. You may only need to have a heart-to-heart talk with a student or you may decide to call the parents, or speak with guidance counselors, social workers, or other administrators. Or, you may decide not to become directly involved, this time, with this student, so that you may continue your teaching at an optimal level: Not every student would necessarily benefit as a result of your intervention.

We advise: If you stretch yourself like a rubberband about to snap, you're overdoing it! No matter how much your heart breaks for a kid in trouble, you must first protect your own ability to function well for all your students. Your own health, your own sanity, your own professional existence is the priority that you must protect above all else. You are neither a trained psychologist nor a social worker; you are a teacher. Whereas you may empathize with your students and their families, your profession is teaching, not psychiatry. Be the best possible teacher by learning to protect your ability to teach well. Teaching is what you do best, and you must safeguard your energy and emotional balance. Know your own limits, and learn to use your school's social support system.

True story: Bill called the home of a student who seemed angry every day in class. The girl refused to answer any questions or participate in class, and she often went to sleep. Bill wanted to ask about the situation at home that was probably affecting his student's behavior. When he called, and a young woman answered the phone, Bill identified himself, named the student, and inquired whether the woman to whom he was speaking was the student's mother. She responded angrily, "Well, if you want to talk about HER, she isn't *my* daughter! You'll have to speak to her father, and he's not home."

Bill never figured out exactly to whom he had been speaking, but he got a new understanding of his student's home situation: complex. Bill felt as if he had wandered into a mine field! Parents often hold teachers responsible for the parents' own unhappiness with their children's (lack of) performance at school.

You can also ask a counselor to ask parents to come into school for a conference with all your students' other teachers, but work with and through the counselor to arrange this massive intervention with parents, other teachers, and the student. Problems with students that concern their whole well-being require more than telephone calls from counselors, and you are well-advised not to take on this responsibility alone. Do not hesitate to ask guidance counselors you trust to make these calls and other arrangements. It is also permissible, and often a good idea, to request that, when these calls are made, the counselor not mention you by name. The guidance counselor can be a buffer between you, your students, and their families.

If your students require any kind of professional referral—medical, psychological, legal, or otherwise—this is the job of the guidance professional. You are overstepping your role if you usurp these tasks, and you will be held accountable if your efforts fail or offend. Failure and offense will jeopardize your ability to function in the classroom, so ask the counselors to take the risks that you sense are necessary.

Some teachers occasionally take professional risks to help their students—Mary (mentioned above) went out on a bit of a limb for her student. Teachers help students write away for college applications; they speak personally to other teachers to ask for extra care for a depressed student; they socialize with students outside of school. Proceed very warily in this area! It is particularly tempting, especially when you are young, single, and independent of family obligations of your own, to undertake rescue missions. You will probably be venturing into areas for which you have not been trained, either formally or by experience: Don't, by trying too hard to be helpful, stand in the way of your student's getting professional help!

YOU, YOUR KIDS, AND THEIR PARENTS

When you speak to parents, whether at your initiative or theirs, do not assume that they know anything at all about your class. Teachers often imagine that their students go home and at the dinner table tell everything that happened to them in school that day. Maybe in the days of Ozzie and Harriet it worked that way, but many American families do not sit down to a family dinner anymore, and it is often hurried and harried when they do. In far too many instances of family non-communication, a parent's innocent question: "What did you do in school today?" is taken as parental prying, and it receives the non-committal response: "*Nuthin.*"

Your phone call may initiate a simple process of merely straightening out misconceptions about what has happened in your class, or it may be blowing the lid off of Pandora's box. Sometimes, teachers try to dominate the conversation in a misguided effort to avoid parental antagonism. All they succeed in doing, however, is reinforcing the near-universal perception of teachers as know-it-alls who "think they know more about my kid than I do." Don't do this! By all means be yourself, but make certain that this includes being cordial and polite.

Be specific about what is expected of students in your class, and how the student in question has performed. Do not agree to change requirements or grading policies when you think this would be inappropriate, but do be patient in offering explanations—the parent you are talking to does not know how school works; you do.

Above all, be understanding, not arrogant: You, not the parents, are the trained teaching professional, and this puts the burden of understanding on your shoulders, not theirs. You're the one who took all those courses on psychology and method and human development; use that knowledge, now, to be helpful to parents who are having problems with their kids.

Listen carefully to discern what kind of a parent you're talking to, so you can put yourself in the parent's shoes. The ideal parent on the other end of the line is this one:

> *I love my kid, I have wonderful dreams of my kid's success in school and in life, and I go to bat for my kid in or out of school whenever I can. Teacher, I hope for only the best for my kid in your class. How can I help?*

Not all parents, however, will give you this positive reply. Other parents will complain to you, wishing that their kid would stop being such a drain on them. Still other parents will react with anxiety or resentment or even hostility when you call: After all, you are calling because there is a problem, aren't you? When does the school ever call to congratulate a parent on doing a swell job of parenting a kid! Some parents, back when they were kids, had difficult experiences with school. They disrespect teachers and hate schools, and they may be totally unsupportive of your efforts. When you pick up that phone to call a kid's home, you are taking your professional life in your hands. Not infrequently, a defensive parent, unwilling to admit that there could be anything wrong with their kid, will take the kid's side against you, making you, the teacher, out to be the bad guy.

Doug, an earnest young math teacher, became distressed because one of his students was doing poorly. When Doug called the student's home, the parent became belligerent and hostile on the phone, wanting to blame the teacher for the student's problems. The kid—unbeknownst to Doug—was listening on another phone; the student came to school the next day with a smirk on his face and gossip on his lips. He told all his friends, "Boy, did my dad give it to Mr. R. last night!" Doug's honest attempt to communicate had become a parent's deceitful entrapment when the student was allowed to eavesdrop on the conversation.

We teachers wish that the parents of our students would be part of the educational team, that they would encourage a love of learning, and that they would foster optimal study conditions at home. If we assume that our wish is a reality, however, we are engaging in dangerous hallucinations. Many parents lack the time or energy or inclination to get involved in their children's school life and work. Especially in these days of finger-pointing over the inadequacies of American public-school education, teachers and parents alike have a natural tendency to hold each other responsible for being unable to solve the problems of their kids.

By all means do complete all written forms that go home to parents, such as mid-term reports and conference reports. The best reports to parents are the most specific and concrete. Rather than reporting that Johnny "tries very hard," you actually do a better job reporting exactly what scores he's earned thus far on tests, quizzes, and class participation. In case you have to deal with an angry parent who wants to blame you for John's problems, hard data is always less loaded and easier to discuss than are vague generalizations about attitude and effort. And, if you have the energy and really want to succeed with your parents, go the extra mile and write positive reports home for your students, too. In these reports, also mention specific papers, test grades, and other particular achievements.

Do parents want to help in handling behavior problems in your classes? Most often they do not. Calls home about poor behavior can weaken your authority both with kid and parents. In most instances, a call for help to the parent is your admission that you have difficulty managing the class.

Some teachers find that a surprise phone call in which parents are informed about poor grades combined with poor behavior can get the kid called onto the carpet with the result of improved performance.

Others, by contrast, find that ominous phone calls from school build fear, whereas face-to-face meetings in which you call on your student for positive behavior are more effective. If you are not sure of the kind of response you may get at a student's home, proceed delicately.

In some schools, parents wield a great deal of clout regarding the decision about your tenure. Some school systems seek parental comments before they award tenure. Many schools receive these opinions whether they request them or not! Your administrators may share with you what parents write or say about you, or they may not. Letters of praise or criticism will occasionally be put in your personnel file. In any event, the impression that your teaching makes through the parents' grapevine will affect your career. A wise teacher assumes that every parent is a member of the School Board—who knows? They may be! Consistency, fairness, clarity, and professional teaching practices will protect you from emotionally unstable parents. Those qualities will also enable you to have positive dealings with parents who truly want the best for their children's academic life.

If you have an upsetting conversation with a parent, it is a good idea to inform your immediate supervisor about it. You may anticipate that there will be a follow-up call about you, so it's better for your supervisor to have heard about the altercation from you, first. In addition, you help your supervisor ahead of time to deal with the situation by supplying the details. Administrators are often quite sympathetic if you have had a bad time with a parent because they deal with irrational or irate parents all the time. If your administrator provides you with advice and support, you will very quickly learn the routine at your school for dealing with unhappy parents. If, however, your administrator blames you and fails to back you up, then you have learned not to share information with your administrators about these unsuccessful conversations with parents. In the future, avoid making calls to parents that may get you in hot water with an unsympathetic administrator. Find another way!

Return calls when parents call you. Usually parents want to inform you about a situation in their home or ask for help or for information concerning their child's progress. Before you call, however, take the precaution of checking with your student's guidance counselor about any situation in the home that you should know about. Guidance counselors are usually willing to give you their opinions of parents. Evaluate what you hear, and act accordingly.

How do you know when to call or write parents besides the usual report cards and written notifications? Generally, if you see something new or unusual in your students' performance, or changes in their attitudes and behaviors that interfere with their performance, you do need to inform their parents.

If you have met parents in person before you call, it is a tremendous advantage to you. If your school has an open-school night in the fall, be sure to pass around a sheet of paper asking parents to sign their names and the names of their children so that you can associate the student with his or her parent(s). If you are able to share a few words with individual parents that night, it will help for you to know whom you are dealing with in future conversations. Parents who expect the school and the teachers to respond immediately to their wishes, can be counted on to attend these functions—but they're the easy ones to work with. Parents who are intimidated by schools, or who feel that the school domain is outside their province, seldom attend—but they're the ones who may need the most to become involved. The most frequent request you will hear from parents on an open-school night is this: "Please call me right away if you see any problems with Johnny." Translate this request to this: "If Johnny is not doing well on his tests, please call me right away so I can do something before it is too late in the term." This type of request is best handled by sending written notices home every three-to-four weeks.

As in all other areas of teaching, learning when to communicate with parents in order to help your students is a longterm, complicated process of learning through experience. You really do deserve congratulations for caring about your students enough to want to get involved, call their parents, and get the parents involved. It means that you have all the right instincts. Therefore, do not blame yourself should you meet with the occasional frosty reception when you call. Many parents will respond warmly and say: "Thank you so much for calling! I know this means you really care." Take heart: It's true—you do!

As you acquire experience with your school, you will have your own collection—like ours—of stories to tell and practical lessons learned. You will be pleasantly surprised by some of the outcomes of your efforts—patience and concern often do pay off. Pace yourself carefully, remain flexible, intervene when you know you can help, but stand aside when you may do damage. While you are teaching your subject you are also dealing with sensitive individuals in a bureaucratic situation.

Whoever said that teaching is easy?

REWARDS

Everyone does what they do in order to be happy; happiness is the reward we all seek. Teaching makes you happy because it is rewarding, but it is rewarding only when you approach it full of imagination and invention. In most cases, the financial rewards of teaching remain inappropriately low. But there are the other rewards—the rewards for inventiveness and imagination in teaching—that are yours both to give yourself and to receive from others.

Teaching can become a tedious chore; teaching the same courses, day after day, year after year, can promote burnout, IF YOU LET IT. The challenge for you is to teach inventively. What people mean when they say that so-and-so is a "good teacher" is that so-and-so is an imaginative teacher. To meet the challenge of being a good teacher, is to understand that teaching is ever-changing: You are ever-changing as a teacher; the academic field of your professional interest (whether early childhood or college-prep physics) is ever-changing; and your students—alive and growing—are ever-changing.

Dragging those same yellowed lesson plans out every semester is stultifying to you and deadly dull for the minds placed in your care. Unfortunately, one of the bitter realities of the teaching profession is that, too often, some teachers do just that—they rely time after time on those old faded notes and plans which were already obsolete after the first time they were tried.

We have both been asked on different occasions by various people the following question: "Why do you continue to work so hard, planning fresh lessons on Sundays, when, after all, you have been teaching for ten years?" Sadly, not only those who do not teach but also many of our teaching colleagues wonder why we work on Sunday afternoons. Many teachers are suspicious of other teachers who work "too hard."

Carl, an experienced teacher we know, was invited to a dinner party by another teacher in his department. Carl declined the invitation; he needed the time to prepare some discussion questions and quizzes. The teacher to whose party he had been invited was miffed that Carl would not attend; she said, "You have taught that novel before on five different occasions; just use your files."

"Just use your files"—four words that will destroy your effectiveness in the classroom! Imagining the inventions that will qualify you for one of the few tangible rewards of teaching—tenure—must not stop after you have attained this plateau of professional comfort. Imagining new approaches and inventing new devices are two of the intangible rewards of teaching that the attainment of tenure gives you the freedom to pursue. This is an ongoing, self-rewarding process that is life-giving and life-sustaining. You earned tenure by exercising your imagination and by being inventive; you continue to deserve tenure the same way.

IMAGINATION AND INVENTION

Why are some teachers called "good" and some called "bad?" What do you remember about the teacher who made a difference in your school career and your life? Why, in fact, do you remember some teachers, but others not at all? One of the common denominators of good teaching is a lively imagination that manifests itself in clever instructional inventions. There are as many ways to be a "good" teacher as there are teacherly imaginations. First, you must have knowledge of your subject. Next, you must prepare a set of logically developed lessons that will help your students master the material. And then, you need some tricks of the trade—motivational devices—to help you spark your daily lessons with playfulness and new chances for students to shine. We include a few of these that have worked for us.

I IS FOR **IMAGINATION** AND **INVENTION**

Birthday Cards

Use birthday cards and a birthday treat—a package of lifesavers or gum—to make each student feel special and noticed in a happy, personal way. A student's birthday is a great day to make personal contact. A meaningful conversation begun on a student's birthday may continue for the remainder of the year.

Go through your class rosters in early September, writing down each student's birthday. Then, organize this information by month, so that you can easily look at the chart as each month begins, prepare the card, and buy the treat for the birthday girl or boy. Write a cheery, happy-birthday greeting on the chalkboard for all the class to see.

Celebrating birthdays works for some teachers, but others find it a burdensome chore which, if forgotten, causes hurt feelings. Once you set up a system like this, you must maintain it; otherwise, you can look foolish and earn a reputation for being scattered. Birthday greetings are a fun idea, but—know thyself!—a regular birthday greeting for each student is not a tactic for the disorganized.

Class Projects

Setting up class projects that are different from the run-of-the-mill "Read the chapter and answer the questions" routine energizes you and your students alike. Role-playing, panel discussions, and debates are possible in all subject areas. Students value lessons that are out-of-the-ordinary; students value teachers who strive to present the material in an innovative manner, especially when the teacher doesn't do all the talking. When you involve your students themselves in planning, directing, and evaluating the projects, they work harder and learn smarter.

After reading *The Scarlet Letter*, by Nathaniel Hawthorne, Carol decided that it would be worthwhile for her students to meet the characters in person to discuss their motivations and desires first-hand. She invited some students to dress as the characters, and she asked them to engross themselves in the characters' personae. Meeting Hester Prynne and Arthur Dimmesdale in the flesh was a real highlight of the year for the class. Carol even used these personal appearances to her own political advantage: She invited her supervisor in on the day of the presentations.

These kinds of "fun and games" are not mere gimmickry, you know. Different people learn in different ways, and not everyone learns best when asked to "read the chapter and answer the questions." We need to take a smorgasbord approach to teaching, such that we spread the table of learning with as many tempting dishes and confections as we can imagine and invent.

Jack, a social-studies teacher new in his school, developed a method of bringing the French Revolution to life for his students, and making a splash for himself as the newcomer. He staged a scenario in which peasants, clergy, and royalty met to discuss the problems and concerns that led to the French Revolution. His students learned the material, assigned their own roles, dressed for the occasion, and excitement—rather than guillotine terror of the final exam—reigned supreme.

Special projects are best when their life-span is short: about a week. Longer than this, and you will begin to feel harried because of the natural restraints of the curriculum. Another reason for keeping activities brief is that too much of a good thing becomes a bad thing. Students need variety, and even the most interesting project becomes deadly if it lasts too long.

Student of the Week/Month

Nothing beats praise for helping your students achieve and learn. Designate a particular student as "Student of the Week" or "Student of the Month." Present an achievement certificate (for genuine achievement), and voilà, you will have your students vying for this reward. The actual certificate needs to be impressive looking, and the award ceremony for the presentation needs to be significant.

As with anything else, the awards approach can have its negative side and could backfire. Announce the standard for success to your students, be consistent in your appeal to these standards, uphold the standards in meting out the award. Display an honor role of the names of those students who have received the award once; find other students to be the recipients in the future. Consistency and organization are crucial, but so is authenticity: Don't "pass it around" just to be democratic, and don't give an achievement award to someone who has not achieved something deserving of reward; otherwise the invention loses its meaning.

Parties

If your students have really been working hard, then you can give them a "good-for-you party." If your students have not been working hard, then you might want to give them a "get-up-and-get-going party." (Any excuse for a party is a good excuse!) Parties can take many forms. Your imagination comes into play here as you define your notion of what a party is.

You can invent a party out of a class project. Promise your students that you will bring them doughnuts and milk if they do extremely well on a test. Promise them that you will conduct the lesson outside on the next nice day. Promise them the reward of a free period if they all perform at a stated level on the next test, and then let them help one another get ready for the test. Use your imagination, and promise them anything, so long as you can deliver, but always promise the party far enough in advance so that they will have time to generate the momentum to win their reward. Announcing a party after the fact is not only ineffective but also less fun because your students will merely be soaking up the milk and doughnuts instead of crowing about their great efforts.

It's probably a good idea to keep within the school rules. (You're new, around here, don't forget! If they sound like they're having too much fun in there, they're probably not learning anything!) Make certain that you can maintain order and discipline in your classroom under party conditions. Define your expectations and make them clear ahead of time with your students to avoid problems.

MOTIVATIONAL TRICKS OF THE TRADE

Students can be bribed. This is a truth that may save your life, or, at least, your lesson. Carrot-and-stick works better with mules than with kids. Meting out zeroes only produces negative results not only in the students' grades but also in their self-esteem and decorum. Giving out zeroes is really unnecessary, particularly in the face of the very positive results that the savvy teacher can achieve with positive reinforcements. Let them eat carrots!

We know of one successful teacher who makes random announcements that particular students will receive a point or two extra for doing some task well. For instance, he may tell Timisha that she just got two points on her quarter grade for coming into class and getting out her materials before the bell rang. Or, he may tell Jason that he got a point for a particularly well-thought-out answer to a discussion question. Or, he may reward an entire row of students for perfect attendance. The element of surprise, together with the knowledge that positive behaviors net positive gains, helps to arrest the attention of students and make them eager to psych out what might earn an extra point or two.

Another fun method is using stickers to reward students whose work is particularly fine. What? Stickers for secondary school students? Gold stars and stickers were all very well in "the grades," but surely not with older kids! Wrong!!! We know a teacher named Devin who had a whole set of rubber stamps—Smiley Faces, Frowny Faces, a turkey, a sunburst, the "Devin Seal of Approval"—that he used effectively in a college computer class. The right stickers, used the right way, will work at any level.

Don't make a big deal of it—don't announce to older kids that they will be working for a dinosaur sticker or an apple or a train. They would rightly laugh and scoff! Surprise them quietly. Attach a colorful sticker to an excellent essay or a well-done quiz, and watch what happens. Even as your students show their dinosaur awards to their peers in a mocking manner, they will be inwardly boasting. You have used your imagination to capture their imaginations! They don't dare put down those dinosaurs too hard, or they'll be putting down their own achievements.

After sticking on a few rounds of job-well-done stickers, Randy got the idea that her students did not appreciate the stickers, so she stopped sticking them on. The outcry, the uproar, the barrage of consternation over the stoppage of the stickers threatened to overturn her control of her class. Randy quickly realized that her teenagers had been enjoying the stickers precisely because everyone thought that they were supposed to be too sophisticated for them. Teens—like the rest of us—

sometimes become nostalgic about their lost childhoods, and they like to be reminded of events and emotions from years and years before. Teach their feelings as well as their minds, and you become a more successful teacher. Stickers are one way of allowing the child within to stay alive.

What about candy? Candy makes a great "carrot," though we prefer it the least of all our motivational methods because it is extrinsic to the learning process. Rewards are best when they are built into the process and its achievement. We prefer to reward an academic job well-done with grade points rather than with a Milky Way; nevertheless, there are times when candy is dandy in the classroom, for younger and older students alike.

Posters and Decorations

The good uses of color are well-known in the elementary school classroom. As you drive by the elementary school in your neighborhood, you can tell what season it is by looking at the windows plastered with construction-paper autumn leaves in the fall, snowflakes in the winter, and flowers in the spring. The visual frame of mind—as every good grade-school teacher knows—is one of the ways we learn.

Too often, the middle-school and secondary-school classroom is visually bleak. Yet advertisers, special-interest groups, performing artists, and many other sources make your access to colorful and stimulating posters free and easy. Posters can provide your students with bits and pieces of wisdom and knowledge that they normally would not pick up or that they might resist in other formats. A drastic poster that graphically shows the effects of drunk driving will get the message across more surely than a long lecture on the dangers of driving while intoxicated. Graphics that similarly explain study methods and other bits of academic lore can supply your students with the potent subliminal messages that will stimulate their studies. Change the posters throughout the year; keep them fresh, colorful, and arresting of the imagination.

Decorate your classroom for the seasons. The change of seasons and the fun of holidays are not just for little kids. Think back to your own elementary school years; one of the things that you remember best is probably the decorations that the teacher posted in your room. It works in middle school and high school equally well. Smiling jack-o'-lanterns and friendly ghosts may work best to enliven the Halloween atmosphere for the little guys, whereas something slightly more ghoulish and ghastly may titillate an older crowd, and tracking the spiritual pilgrimage of the "Peanuts" people as they await the rising of the Great Pumpkin may appeal to sophisticates, but in every classroom—just as in every restaurant and bar, shopping mall and church in the adult world—color, decoration, and seasonal trimmings are part of marketing the product. Your product happens to be knowledge, but the marketing strategies are the same.

Our students' favorite decorations have always been those we put up for Halloween and Valentine's Day. One October 31st, Ken brought little finger-goblin puppets to class and announced to his students that the ghosts were former students of his whom he had transformed because they hadn't done their work. The all-time best day on the calendar for literature teachers is February 14th—the day that every lusty teenager's thoughts turn poetic. Hearts and flowers, sonnets and blank verse: The poetry teacher who can't figure out a way to make Valentine's Day work as an instructional motivator to high literacy is being neither imaginative nor inventive.

Be careful here of your students' sensibilities and of areas of "political correctness." Avoid posters that might be perceived as supportive of a particular political party, ideological persuasion, or religious tradition, unless you conscientiously assemble a collection of posters for comparative purposes, in which case a sample from any quarter is allowable as educational. As your class gets ready for Election Day, for example, put up not only Democrat and Republican posters but also Libertarian, Socialist, and other third-party posters, and posters on all sides of all issues. The American classroom is the free marketplace of ideas. Only you, the teacher, need maintain professional neutrality.

N IS FOR NEUTRALITY

Group Work

Kids—like grown-ups—love to talk. Let this need work for you, not against you, in your classes. Divide students into groups, and have them work collectively on assignments. Our ancestors knew about it on the frontier, tribal societies know it well, and American education has recently been rediscovering the practicality of collaborative/cooperative learning. Giving one grade to the entire group will ensure not only that they all work hard but also that they will help one another to learn. Instead of one teacher teaching 30 students, you will have 31 teachers teaching one another. Peer pressure is a powerful tool in any case, and it is a powerful tool for good when you can channel it towards learning.

Even exams can be given to groups of students and taken collaboratively. The collective test is often effective, energizing, different, and highly instructive. Anything out of the ordinary, anything that sets the class off as different from the others, anything that gets your students to talking and thinking, will help your lessons succeed.

The Point System

Even the most unwilling scholar among your students sooner or later will succumb to the seduction of extra points. Sooner or later, the piper must be paid, and all students want to graduate. How can you capitalize on this fatal attraction imaginatively and invent a point system that will serve you as a high-powered engine of learning? Kids understand the concrete, the specific, and the clearly stated. Moreover, we repeat, they are susceptible to bribery. The grade "A+" is the ultimate carrot. If you deliver grades to your students on a fair, rational, utterly reliable, and previously agreed-upon contractual basis—"this grade for that amount of performance"—it will guarantee learning achievement for them and teaching success for you.

As a new teacher, it may be that you've never used a point system before, and don't know how. Here are some tips that we have accumulated through the years: In a point system, you establish how many points are possible during the term if a student were to make 100 percent on every piece of graded work. Then, at grade time, you add up all the points that a student has made during the grading period, get a total, and establish a ratio. For example, if a total of 600 points was possible, and a given student racked up 450 points, then you calculate the grade according to this formula: $100/600 = X/450$.

Novice teachers often assume that a point system takes an immense amount of time, but, in fact, this is not the case: It takes a while to invent a reliable point system, but after it's in place, you can easily revise it and adapt it to many class situations. Grading time goes quickly, and all you need is a hand-held calculator and a clear statement of how many points were possible.

Moreover, the point system holds advantages that no other system can boast: The point system prevents your having to hear the common complaints—both from students and from their parents—that someone did not deserve the grade they got.

Another advantage of the point system is that you can bribe your students very easily. If a major exam is worth, say, 200 points, tell them that they can make up for lost points with particularly brilliant performance—worth, say, 5 points—during class discussion. Or, tell them that an extra-credit assignment is worth a quiz of, say, 50 points. Students want to succeed, and they need only fair and clear opportunities to do so.

A further advantage of the point system, especially when you treat it like a negotiated contract, is that it involves your students in both the planning and the evaluation phases of their learning—and that's good instruction. When you are setting up your point system, invite your students' participation: What projects are they willing to undertake? How many points ought to be given for this quiz or that exam or the other report? What do they want to learn from taking this class, what are they willing to do to learn it, and what would they consider a fair evaluation of their performance to be?

When you establish your grade-point contract with them on this negotiated basis, they feel like the adults that they so want to become because you have treated them like adults, allowing them to have some say in, some ownership of, this work of schooling that so affects their lives. You have treated them like peers, co-learners, welcoming their input, and working with them collaboratively "from below," rather than imposing half-understood, wholly resented structures on them "from above" in an authoritarian manner. You have, in fact, modeled democracy in an educationally built-in way, rather than merely teaching a civics lesson from the textbook.

A way to surprise and gratify your students, even as they work within your point system, is to offer unexpected help to get them ready for exams. Prepare freebies (no points given, none taken), sample tests that teach test-taking skills at the same time that they teach what is needed on the for-points test. Let them see copies of old finals; that way they learn what to expect (test formats, styles of questions) and how to proceed (pacing themselves during timed exams, when to guess and when not) when it comes time to sit down to take the real test. Nothing relieves test-anxiety better than preparing for new tests by practicing on old ones. Make a game out of taking old tests so that your students can see how they are progressing, without the threat of a grade hanging over them.

The purposes to be accomplished when getting your students ready for a test is to motivate them to study, inspire them to achieve, and empower them to succeed. Avoid the deadly re-teaching of long lists of terms and concepts, a technique that either builds anxiety or grinds on in deadly boredom. Instead, capitalize on the activities that have proved to be successful learning experiences for your students. Teach them (as you did when setting up your point system) to design a clear-cut and well-organized study program of review through which they can proceed at a reasonable pace. Show them how to organize what they know for finals and other exams by demonstrating how to organize, review, recall, and thereby make manageable what seems to them to be an unclimbable mountain of material. End your units of study (and the whole teaching year) with energy and organization, and your students will reward you with greater success and achievement.

Be wise: Be consistent. If you start with a point system, stick with it; don't give it up midstream. Aim for clarity in your grade book, reliability in your application of the agreed-upon standards, and fairness in your assessments. Consistency, clarity, and efficient organization are crucial to your success as a grader, just as they are essential to your success overall as a teacher.

Be honest and truthful about the grades you give, what they mean, how you arrived at them, and what use you make of them. Because students have an amazing ability to deny their own poor performances, and imagine that they are doing well in spite of incomplete homework and nodding off in class, they need the reality of fair tests to ground them. Do not disguise bad grades by vague comments. Often and repeatedly, be clear about what is expected. Do give your students endless opportunities to make new beginnings, whether on the next unit, the next paper, or the next discussion the next day.

Why is it that when a teacher gives formal grades, some students will work hard, while others become discouraged and give up?

But why is it that when teachers don't give formal grades, some students will stop working and learning altogether?

The struggle between trying to generate internal energy and interest within some students while being forced to levy it externally on others by wielding the red pen is an unavoidable dilemma of teaching. It can be made a little easier for the new teacher who is willing to contemplate students as individuals. The carrot-and-stick of tests and grades works well for the majority; however, your discernment, patience, imagination, and invention are required for students who need a different style of motivation. The net effect for everyone involved is happiness in the classroom.

The Weekly Division

We asked some new teachers who had achieved success and happiness during that first year what quality or qualities had given them their initial good fortune. Over and over again, we heard that they had divided their week into manageable, discrete units, and that they had been consistent in maintaining this routine.

This is the chapter on imagination and invention, not rhythms, so it may seem odd to discuss routines; nonetheless, routines can be liberating, and in liberation lies the freedom to be inventive. Rather than worrying: "Oh dear, today is Tuesday! Whatever shall I do today?" you will know that it is Tuesday, and that Tuesday is your collaborative group day. You are then free to put your energies into planning the lesson within that framework, rather than having to imagine a new framework at the same time that you are inventing a new lesson. In disciplined freedom, you can be innovative and organized at the same time. Students need routines, too, especially at the lower levels, and even upperclassmen value structure, though they rebel against it, and they will reimpose it upon themselves, given the opportunity.

Some people would disagree, arguing that imagination and inventiveness are lost within structure and routine. **We advise:** You can allow for flexibility within your system of weekly division, just as you can allow for grading flexibility within your point system. Build flexibility itself into whatever systems you devise, whether planning and dividing, or assessing and grading. During your teaching day, instant and inventive decision-making is a skill you will need to call upon to cope with all manner of unforeseen developments. Structure does not necessarily negate invention, nor invention, structure; they build upon one another. Similarly, discipline and imagination do not necessarily impede one another; without discipline, imagination remains fuzzy and helpless, and without imagination, discipline becomes a rigor like death. Finding your own balance of innovation and routine is part of teaching your way to success.

THE BEST GIFTS OF ALL

We both love to teach, and we have found many rewards in teaching over the years. The majority of the rewards, however, are those we discovered for ourselves. If you depend on an extrinsic reward system, then you may find the pickings slim. When you discover the rewards that are rewarding in and for themselves, then you become wealthy indeed.

How can you become the teacher you always wanted to be? How can you avoid the quagmire of self-deprecation that has sucked the high-minded idealism out of so many who have gone before you? How can you find the rewards that are, in fact, waiting for you, if you know where to look? Perhaps even more important than the "how" is the "where." Where are the rewards to be found that we assert are there waiting for you?

Develop Friendships

Friendships among teachers are possible, and real collegiality is one of the plusses of teaching. Both of us have developed genuine friendships over the years, both early in our careers and even more recently. Friendship among teaching colleagues tends to develop slowly, however, for various occupationally hazardous reasons. At every turn, we advise you to be cautious in forging associations. Expecting too much, offering too much too soon, may lead to real disappointment.

A resilient cohesion of mind and spirit is possible among people in a school, similar to the dynamics of an old-fashioned extended family. It works like this: You are all in the same boat experiencing similar problems, similar victories, similar disappointments. Sometimes you will get angry with each other, sometimes you will be happy, but through it all is the feeling of the oneness of common purpose and common love of the kids that permeates the relationship.

Two sources of possible friendship at school are mentors and peer coaches. (See "Systems" for our discussion of mentors and peer coaches.) A good mentor or a peer coach can do a lot to reduce the real sense of isolation and the early confusion of the new teacher. The warm and trusting response that will naturally rise in you out of gratitude for being treated cordially and collegially in your new environment may tend to flow onward towards friendship, if your mentor or peer coach is available to become a long-term friend. One problem with looking for a friend in your mentor is that, usually, the age difference is greater between mentor and mentee. This has little impact upon the efficacy of the mentoring process itself, but it can tend to obstruct the formation of a friendship. For your own part, be prepared for your mentor or peer coach to take a somewhat more businesslike attitude towards mentoring and coaching you. For them, it may be just a part of the job. If so, don't let it hurt your feelings. Find your friend elsewhere.

We advise: Make friends with your teaching peers, but do not expect to be friends with your students. You are a grown-up, and they are kids; you're their teacher, not their equal. Even if they are graduating high-school seniors and you are just out of college, the four years that separate you are—and need to continue to be—the border that marks a generation gap. No matter how young and vigorous you think yourself to be, no matter how much you want to be their pal, understand that your students see in you first and foremost a figure of authority. Similarly, you are neither the mommy nor the daddy of your younger students. Keep your relationship with your students of all ages cordial but professional. Friendships can, and indeed they do, happen between teacher and student, but they are laid on a foundation of separation that must be firmly in place before a healthy alliance can begin to build.

Victories

Certain victories will be yours as you march through your teaching career. Recognize them when they appear, and savor each and every one of them. *Carpe diem!* "Seize the day" and each day's victories, and enjoy them!

You have taught a wonderful lesson, and Brad has finally understood what you have been trying to get across to him and the 29 others. He has produced an insightful paper; give it back to him with a smile, but before you do so, photocopy it! His paper reflects both the quality of work of which he was capable and the effort, time, and intelligence that you poured out to teach him the research skills.

You have gone above and beyond the call of duty for Susan, who had been having a difficult time with her mother; you sat down and talked with both of them, and you have effected a change in their relationship. Now, Susan's mother has written a note to the principal thanking you publicly for your assistance. The principal—bless him!—has written you a note congratulating you on your ability to touch the lives of your students and their parents. Save those notes!

You have had a wonderful class; it has been a serendipitous year; June has busted out all over, and you need to say farewell. Often, this is a particularly traumatic moment for the new teacher. Here's a way to reward yourself while saying good-bye with a gentle flair: Take snapshots of the kids, and assemble a rogues' gallery of your successes (and sweetly remembered near-misses). We learned this technique from an old colleague and friend of ours who was retiring; he was really saddened by his upcoming retirement, but he recognized the reality of the situation. Rather than complain and moan, he took pictures of his last-hurrah classes that year, and not only did he make copies for himself but also he mailed pictures to all his students. It was his way of separating graciously and of saying a gentle good-bye.

Your students have completed a project, and it has gone well; your goals have been met, and you and they are proud of the work they have done. Get out your camera! Take snapshots of the students at work, take snapshots of their work, and post it all on the bulletin boards. Too often, the bulletin boards become tired and old. Change them frequently and deck them out with the students' own work and faces.

In teaching, the victories frequently do not occur immediately after the struggle. Indeed, this delay happens more often than not. Any school teacher can tell you about his or her surprise when Chris or Tamika popped by two or three—or five or ten—years later to say: "What a wonderful teacher you were!" If you turn out to be the kind of teacher that the kids all gossip about as "tough," but whom they remember fondly all their lives, you will have received a great reward—even though, in some cases, you will never know it.

Take Courses

New teachers, right out of college, are often probationary until they get their Master's degrees. Taking courses to complete these requirements is important and necessary, but it need not be a burden. Think of coursework as one of your rewards! Take courses that you like; look for programs that are rewarding for you. In most cases, guidelines tend to be fairly broad on which courses you are allowed to take towards permanent certification.

You are going to be working hard the first few years of your teaching career; if you do not enjoy the courses that you will be taking, then you will be at a considerable disadvantage. Don't stress yourself; take one course per term. Yes, it is good to finish your Master's as soon as you can, but you also need to be alive at the end of the pro-gram to accept the degree!

After your Master's degree, most districts give you credit for additional coursework beyond the Master's. Each credit that you earn puts you on the path to a higher salary. Find courses that enrich your life, either professionally or personally. Often, districts will give you credit for workshops or professional meetings that you attend. Districts may also give you inservice credit for writing an article or a book. There are myriad ways to earn credits and achieve success and happiness in teaching. Seek, and ye shall find!

Buy Yourself What You Need

Workers are worthy of their tools. Don't scrimp!

Too often, teachers find themselves constrained by budgets over which they have no control, into which they have no input. Videos, teaching aids, books not on the list, cannot be purchased because of a tight budget. One of the ways to get around this budgetary frustration is simply to buy for yourself what you need with your own money.

Smart teachers do not depend on others for what they can do themselves. Buy the things that you want and need. You will be happier not only because you will be in control of your surroundings but also because you will have the items you want and the work power that they afford you. A plus here is that professional purchases may be tax-deductible.

Buy what you need and want, but—the same rule that applies elsewhere is in force here, too—do so quietly. Some of your colleagues or your supervisors may not look favorably upon you if you have teaching aids that have not been stamped "officially approved" by the powers that be. In fact, many supervisors do not value teaching aids at all; they argue that it's good for new teachers to do everything themselves. But why—we reply—should you have to reinvent the educational wheel? If there are excellent tests on the market that your district does not provide, then buy them yourself, and put your energies to work in other areas. When you purchase aids, equipment, and supplies, you buy yourself some time. You can put this extra time to work in other areas where time cannot be so easily acquired. You will feel happier, because you are in control.

Buy wisely and buy well; recognize excellence; you never go wrong with high quality. There are many shoddy teaching materials on the market today. Use any aids that you do purchase prudently and with care; share these materials with those who, you think, will understand and appreciate your effort to "go the extra mile."

Susan was a first-year teacher who photocopied a lot of materials for her students. She was distressed when she discovered that her students were losing these papers because they merely folded them and stuck them into their textbooks. She wanted a heavy-duty hole punch, so that the papers could be snapped into her students' notebooks easily and immediately. When Susan's supervisor refused to purchase the hole-punch for her, she bought one for herself and kept it in her desk to render the handouts immortal. The technique worked; the papers stayed in the notebooks; Susan felt like a success—all for the price of a hole punch which, as far as we know, she is still using.

The "P.S." to this tale is that Susan went quietly about her business, telling no one about her private hole-punch purchase. The next time the supervisor came in to observe Susan, she was really impressed by the students' notebooks. Susan mentioned what she had done, and suddenly, the very next day, a hole punch appeared in the faculty room for the department's use. The supervisor was the heroine of the day.

Maintain Your Self-Worth

People will believe the persona that you develop for yourself. Build your professional image the right way, and you will shine in others' eyes. Deprecate yourself often enough, and others will come to believe that you are worthy of the low image that you project.

In teaching, as in any career, you need to set the stage for yourself and then live out the role in which you have cast yourself. The problem is that teaching is looked down upon by many. Too often, you won't need to put yourself down; others will do it for you.

W IS FOR WORTH

A brother of a teacher we know called her up to tell her some "terrible news": His daughter, her niece, who was attending an Ivy League school had chosen teaching as a career, and here he was, throwing away his money on a preparatory course for teachers at an expensive school that could have been taken at State College. Our friend was horrified: Not only was her own brother putting her and her career choice down but also he was looking for her to commiserate with him regarding his daughter's *dreadful* decision. Even your own family members will sometimes say (and not always behind your back): "What an intelligent person, and to think, you went into teaching!"

What do you say to a guy like that? Throughout this book, we have written about your political need to stand tall and keep silent about your achievements. If all of that is good advice, how can one achieve feelings of dignity and self-worth if one is not free to do a little crowing?

Angela, a math teacher with but two years of experience, confessed to her class that she had never really understood a particular kind of problem. She was hoping that her own "humility" would encourage her students to work harder, but Angela's attempt to be "one of the boys" backfired when her class decided that she really didn't know too much about math. From that point on, a serious tug-o'-war for control of the class began with that group of kids.

People tend to believe your presentation of yourself. You can reward yourself ahead of time by going into teaching with a solid-gold estimation of your own talents and abilities. You don't know everything—you know that, your students know that, your colleagues and your superiors know that. But you do know what you know, you know how to find out what you don't know, and you know how to deliver: That's why you paid all that money and spent all that time and effort learning how to teach. Don't sell yourself short! Dignity and understanding from others will be yours, if you first give them to yourself.

Cultivate Your Life Out of School

Your career is important, and your commitment to it must be clear, definite, and certain during the school day. After the last bell has rung, after the last student has reluctantly (!) left your room, then your other life resumes.

"What other life?" you ask. "What about all the grading, planning, filing, photocopying, reading, and other paperwork that I have to do?" you ask. "I have to go right home and keep working, if my lessons, papers, files, handouts, and reports are to be ready by tomorrow!" you affirm.

The reality is that you will not be able to keep up this constant gallop for long. Sooner or later, you are going to tire. The experienced jockey knows that he must pace his horse well to win the race, and you must move forward into your teaching career pacing yourself with a similar savvy, if you are to stay the course.

You will win no points for being a workaholic—you'll only load yourself up with unnecessary stress. Betty, a first-year science teacher, was constantly working in her lab, setting up the next day's experiments, grading papers, doing all the things that she thought she must do. She often stayed after school for two hours at a clip; she worked right through lunch, and she seemed to have no life other than her job. She developed no real relationships with her colleagues; rather, she never really got acquainted. As the year progressed, Betty became tired and irritable with everyone. She was unpleasant to be around, and she began to lose control of her classes. When hiring time came that spring, Betty was not asked to return the next September. Bright and knowledgeable, hard-working and conscientious, Betty had real potential, but she had failed to develop the other sides of her life, both personal and professional. To be a good teacher means to be a healthy and whole person. You're in that classroom not only for what you know but also for who you are.

Many conscientious new teachers do feel that they have to show their devotion to their students and their jobs 24 hours a day. One way to take this pressure off yourself is to join school committees that interest you. Your efforts will be appreciated, and you will be rewarded by your development of that other side of your professional life.

There are meetings to develop new schedules, there are meetings to discuss school discipline, and there are meetings to plan social occasions, to name a few . These committees may do for you what outside activities can do: They can provide you with parallel outlets for your energies in addition to the actual teaching of your subject and your students, but because they are more sociable, they also provide refreshment and relief from the daily grind. What's more, join the Parent-Teacher Association; get to know the parents of your students in a social setting. After you have tenure, we recommend that you get involved with your teachers' union.

You must be committed to your job, but you must also be committed to yourself. Whatever you do, whether it is joining school committees, becoming the sponsor of an after-school students' club or other special group, working out physically, going to movies or concerts, do something that doesn't require you to hold a piece of chalk. If you keep your life healthy and vital outside of the narrow walls of your classroom, you will enjoy the life that you lead within those walls with greater gusto and contentment, not to mention success.

Forgive Yourself

Reward yourself with forgiveness. Be understanding of your mistakes, and let them become occasions for growth. When you make a mistake—if you lose patience with a student, if your lesson falls flat, if you leave stuff at home that you absolutely politively needed at school—remember Scarlett O'Hara's refrain: "Tomorrow *is* another day." Forgive yourself for today, and meet tomorrow with freshness and newness. You know how liberating it is to forgive someone else; you know how grateful you feel when someone else truly forgives you. Now, make yourself grateful and free by forgiving yourself regularly!

THE MOST IMPORTANT REWARD OF ALL: Your Students

We have asked many teachers—new ones, veterans, young ones, at all levels and in all kinds of schools—this question: "What is it about teaching that you enjoy the most?" Both implicitly and explicitly, the answer that runs consistently through their answers is the pleasure, both extrinsic and intrinsic, that they receive from their students.

Extrinsic rewards that you can expect from your students are those concrete affirmations of your worth as a teacher: their statements of appreciation—"Thanks, Teacher!" "Yo, Teach, you're the greatest!" "She's tough!" "You're the best teacher I ever had." And if your students are singing your praises in this fashion, so will their parents and your administrators also. Unfortunately, explicit, vocal rewards like these are often few and far between. Most of the time, you have to content yourself with the intrinsic pleasures that you derive from your students, which are easier to attain because you can reach for them yourself, without waiting for others to respond.

Among the intrinsic rewards that await you are these:

- The student who, at last, begins to ask insightful questions after sitting for weeks or months, in your class, saying nothing

- The student who, through multiple re-writes, eventually learns how to write a well-developed essay

- The student who finally stops resisting your nightly homework assignments

Accolades, re-hiring, raises, promotions, and tenure are the obvious and extrinsic rewards of teaching without which the name "career success" cannot be given, but these other, intrinsic, silent rewards are the soul-sustaining marks of that other kind of professional success that the true-hearted teacher seeks. Without them, you would quit; with them, you are happy; they are there, or we would not be here.

According to the old Frank Sinatra lyric, "Love and marriage go together like a horse and carriage:...You can't have one without the other." It's the same way with teachers and kids: no students, no teachers. Just as students are the reasons for your being there, so also are students the sources of your ultimate rewards as a teacher. Enjoy your students, and you'll be more than merely a school survivor. Enjoy your students, take your rightful rewards, and you will know what it means to become a successful teacher.

X, Y, AND

Index

Great Resources for Teachers

Becoming a Teacher: A Practical and Political School Survival Guide
by Robin Grusko and Judy Kramer
G46; $14.95

> "Teachers talk about how different the reality of teaching is from the education they received. That . . . is the reason Grusko and Kramer wrote their guide. In college, teachers are taught "kiddie lit" and physical education, but not how to create an office, keep records, or cope with all the demands imposed by children and fellow staff members."
>
> —*Booklist*
> (September 1993)

Peer Teaching and Collaborative Learning in the Language Arts
by Elizabeth McAllister
G13; $15.95

> "Combines the two strategies of peer teaching and collaborative learning in a novel way that holds the promise of success for any classroom."
>
> —*Reading Today*
> (April/May 1991)

A Commitment to Critical Thinking
by Carl B. Smith
G24; $9.95

Promotes critical thinking in the reading classroom through use of an anticipation-reaction guide, a structured text preview, and a study guide combining the "close reading," "historical-critical," and "reader response" approaches to interpretation. Includes 30 classroom activities.

Quiet Children and the Classroom Teacher (Second Edition)
by James McCroskey and Virginia Richmond
G27; $9.95

Shows the teacher how to communicate with quiet students and how to draw them out without causing them to dive deeper into their "communication apprehension."

Teacher Effectiveness and Reading Instruction
by Richard D. Robinson
G25; $14.95

Robinson is at his best as a practical consultant helping reading teachers take specific steps towards becoming more effective. With a checklist of practices he guides the reading teacher through an assessment of attitudes towards sensible application of research results. The extensive, annotated bibliography richly documents the resources.

Designed by teachers

TEACHING RESOURCES IN THE ERIC DATABASE

TRIED

Each volume contains alternatives to textbook teaching. The acronym TRIED reflects the reliability of these hands-on, how-to instructional designs: ideas that have been tried and tested by other teachers, reported in the ERIC database, and now redesigned to be teacher-easy and student-friendly.

Each chapter is organized to make classroom implementation easy:

- **BRIEF DESCRIPTION** — Outlines the focus and content of each chapter's instructional design.
- **SOURCE** — Indicates where to find the original document in the ERIC database.

- **OBJECTIVE** — Notes students' goals for the lesson.
- **PROCEDURES** — Clearly details the steps to be taken.
- **RESULTS** — Projects the outcome of the lesson.

In addition, each TRIED resource book contains:

- **ACTIVITIES CHART** — Cross-references, classroom strategies, and activities in use from chapter to chapter.
- **USER'S GUIDE** — Clearly summarizes the book's organization and focus.

- **ANNOTATED BIBLIOGRAPHY** — Provides citations and abstracts of related resources in the ERIC database

Choose from these 13 Titles in the TRIED Series:

Teaching Literature Written by Women
Expands literature-based learning to include important works of 29 women. Strategies develop respect for gender equity and teach the novels, stories, and poems of Madeline L'Engle, Maya Angelou, Anne Frank, and other women of the past and present. (Elem/Mid/Sec)
T14; $16.95

Teaching Values through Teaching Literature
Presents teaching strategies for today's most powerful instructional materials, including novels, folk literature, poetry, and ethnic literature. Features a section on setting up a program in values clarification through literature. (Mid/Sec)
T13; $16.95

. . . for teachers!

Reading and Writing across the High School Science and Math Curriculum
Contains exciting reading and writing alternatives to the textbook approach. Explore lessons on "writing to learn" in math and science: journal writing, scientific poetry writing, and using writing to overcome those dreaded "story problems." (Sec)
T12; $16.95

Celebrate Literacy! The Joy of Reading and Writing
Covers the full range of language-arts skills and literature to turn your elementary school into a reading and writing carnival including literacy slumber parties, book birthdays, and battles of the books. (Elem)
T11; $14.95

Working with Special Students in English/Language Arts
Helps take the worry out of teaching special students. Strategies to organize your classroom; use computers; implement cooperative learning; and teach thinking skills, reading, and writing to students with special needs. (Elem/Mid/Sec)
T10; $14.95

A High School Student's Bill of Rights
Invites middle and high school students to explore the U.S. Constitution and other bodies of law. Lesson approaches are focused on precedent-setting legal cases that have dealt with student's rights when they were contested in the school context. May be used as a whole course, a mini-course, or as supplementary activities. (Mid/Sec)
T09; $14.95

Reading Strategies for the Primary Grades
Presents a storehouse of clever ideas to begin reading and writing, and to build vocabulary and comprehension. Use stories, poems, response logs, oral reading, Whole Language, and much more! (Elem)
T08; $14.95

Language Arts for Gifted Middle School Students
Supplies challenging lessons in a variety of language-arts areas; communication skills, literature, mass media, theater arts, reading, writing. Activities designed for gifted students also work for others. (Mid)
T07; $14.95

Remedial Reading for Elementary School Students
Uses games and reading activities to stimulate imagination, develop reading skills, and strengthen comprehension. (Elem)
T05; $14.95

Writing Exercises for High School Students
Motivates students to explore creative, and expository writing. Introduces the young writer to all the basics of good writing. (Sec)
T04; $14.95

Critical Thinking, Reading, and Writing
Encourages reading, writing, and thinking in a critically reflective, inventive way for students at all levels. Practical classroom activities make critical thinking an achievable goal. (Elem/Mid/Sec)
T03; $14.95

Teaching the Novel
Offers strategies for teaching many novels, including *To Kill a Mockingbird*, *The Color Purple*, *The Scarlet Letter*, and other oft-taught works of interest to middle school and high school students. (Mid/Sec)
T02; $14.95

Writing across the Social Studies Curriculum
Provides examples of how to connect writing activities with lessons on important topics in the social studies—a writing across the curriculum approach. (Mid/Sec)
T01; $14.95

Order Information

☎ To order by phone, call toll-free **1-800-925-7853** and use your VISA or MasterCard.

✉ To order books by mail, fill out the form below and send to:
ERIC/EDINFO Press
P. O. Box 5247, Dept. G46
Bloomington, IN 47407

Qty.	Title	Order No.	Unit Cost	Total
			Subtotal	
	Shipping & Handling $3.00 for the first book plus $1.00 for each additional book.		Shipping & Handling	
	Method of Payment ❑ check ❑ money order ❑ Master Card ❑ Visa		IN residents add 5% sales tax	
			TOTAL	

Card holder_____

Card no. _____

Expiration date _____

Send books to:

Name _____

Address _____

City_____State _____ Zip _____

Prices subject to change.